TWAYNE'S WORLD AUTHORS SERIES

A Survey of the World's Literature

SPAIN

Alfonso Martínez de Toledo

TWAS 398

¶ Arcipreste de
Talavera que habla delos
vicios delas malas mu
geres: y comple
xiones delos hō
bres.:.

Title Page from *Arcipreste de Talavera*
(Seville: Andrés de Burgos, 1547)

ALFONSO MARTÍNEZ DE TOLEDO

By E. MICHAEL GERLI
Georgetown University

TWAYNE PUBLISHERS
A DIVISION OF G. K. HALL & CO., BOSTON

First Printing

Library of Congress Cataloging in Publication Data

Gerli, E Michael.
Alfonso Martínez de Toledo.

(Twayne's world authors series ; TWAS 398 : Spain)
Bibliography: pp. 175–78
Includes index.
1. Martínez de Toledo, Alfonso, 1398?–1466.
PQ6412.M7Z65 868'.2'07 76–4556
ISBN 0–8057–6239–6

MANUFACTURED IN THE UNITED STATES OF AMERICA

For M

Contents

About the Author

E. Michael Gerli is Assistant Professor of Spanish literature at Georgetown University. He received his B.A. and Ph.D. degrees from the University of California at Los Angeles. His M.A. degree was earned at Middlebury College in Madrid.

Professor Gerli has participated in national and international colloquia, and is the author of numerous scholarly articles on Spanish, Portuguese, and Spanish-American literature. He is presently preparing a critical anthology of pro- and antifeminist medieval Castilian literature, and an edition of Martínez de Toledo's *Atalaya de las crónicas.*

Preface

In keeping with the objectives of the Twayne World Authors Series, I have attempted to provide a survey of the life and works of Alfonso Martínez de Toledo, one of Spain's important, but neglected, literary geniuses of the late Middle Ages. In this effort I have concentrated on the *Arcipreste de Talavera o Corbacho* (*Archpriest of Talavera or Whip*), Martínez's most important, most well-known, and most readily available work.

The analysis of the *Archpriest of Talavera* (Chapters 2 through 6) endeavors to point out its principal sources, how these were dealt with, and the artistic consequences of their use. In the course of this study, I have naturally touched upon subjects that in themselves deserve more attention than could possibly be given in one book. This is the case, for example, with the amatory philosophy expressed in the *Corbacho*—its roots in the Augustinian tradition, its interpretations in medieval Spain (especially in the *Libro de buen amor*), its relationship to the condemnations of courtly love, and finally, its effect upon Martínez de Toledo himself. In addition, much more could be said about the work's textual problems, its antifeminism, and the impact of pulpit oratory on its themes, style, and structure.

In Chapter 7 I have dealt somewhat summarily with Martínez's other works. This was intentional. Although the *Atalaya de las crónicas* (*Watchtower of the Chronicles*) is very important, it still remains only in manuscript form. I have therefore limited my discussion of it to a brief description of the manuscripts, their content, sources, and intent, and some aspects of its literary interest. The *Vidas de San Ildefonso y San Isidoro* (*Lives of San Ildefonso and San Isidoro*) are minor compositions that in fact amount to little more than a pastiche of Latin hagiographies. Hence, I have only pointed out their sources and some of Martínez's individual contributions to them. Two works once attributed to Martínez, the *Invencionario* (*Book of the Inventors of All Things*) and the *Vencimiento del mundo* (*Vanquishment of the World*), are not discussed. Raúl del Piero's studies on these (see Bibliography) and recent biographical findings obviate the need to do so: they could not have been written by Martínez de Toledo.

Although there is really no adequate substitute for the original Spanish, I have used Lesley Byrd Simpson's masterful translation of the *Corbacho*. His English version captures admirably the tone, subtleties, and levels of Martínez's work. My only regret is that Professor Simpson did not see fit to translate Part IV of the *Archpriest of Talavera*. All translations from the fourth part, therefore, are mine.

I wish to express my sincere gratitude to a number of people who have all in some way contributed to this study. First, I am most deeply indebted to Professor D. W. Lomax for providing me with a copy of his forthcoming "Datos biográficos sobre el Arcipreste de Talavera." Without his important discoveries, Chapter 1 would indeed have been deficient. Next, I wish to thank Miss Christine J. Whitbourn for allowing me to quote from her recent noteworthy study on the Archpriest. If my conclusions differ from hers and Professor Lomax's, I beg tolerance. I am also especially grateful to Professor Julio Rodríguez-Puértolas, friend and mentor, for his perceptive insights and intelligent suggestions on an early draft of the manuscript. Moreover, I gratefully acknowledge Professor Paul C. Smith for his advice and keen observations. And special thanks to my wife, Merete, for her patient criticism and encouragement. Finally, I wish to extend my sincere appreciation to Professor Gerald E. Wade, former Spanish editor for Twayne's World Authors Series, for giving me the opportunity to write *Alfonso Martínez de Toledo*.

* * * *

After these lines were written, a newly published critical edition of the *Corbacho* came to my attention: Alfonso Martínez de Toledo, *Arcipreste de Talavera*, critical edition by Marcella Ciceri, 2 volumes (Modena, Italy: Società Tipografica Editrice Modenese, 1975). Volume I contains the text. Volume II contains an introduction, a list of textual variants, a valuable glossary, and an index. See my forthcoming review in the *Nueva Revista de Filología Hispánica* (1977).

Chronology

1398 Alfonso Martínez de Toledo is born in Toledo.

1406 Reign of Juan II of Castile begins.

1412 In accordance with the provisions of the Compromise of Caspe (1410), Fernando de Antequera is crowned Fernando I of Aragon. Death of Françesc Eiximenis.

1415 Martínez de Toledo holds a prebendary in the Chapel of Ancient Kings in Toledo Cathedral.

1419 Juan II of Castile declared of age. Death of Saint Vincent Ferrer.

1424 Martínez de Toledo litigates with Fernán García for archpriestship of Talavera de la Reina. Death of Alfonso Alvarez de Villasandino, foremost poet of the *Cancionero de Baena* (*Baena's Songbook*).

1427 Martínez de Toledo challenged for archpriestship of Talavera by Francisco Fernández. Fernández writes to Pope Martin V accusing Martínez de Toledo of cohabiting with a woman. The Archpriest leaves Castile for Crown of Aragon. In Barcelona he experiences the great earthquakes. While there he probably comes under the protection of Juan de Casanova, the future Cardinal San Sixto.

1430 Casanova named Cardinal and Bishop of Gerona by Martin V. With the newly appointed cardinal's help, Martínez obtains the promise of an additional benefice in Toledo Cathedral.

1431 The Archpriest litigates against the deacon of Toledo, Domingo González, in order to maintain a recently acquired prebendary. He goes to Rome to present his case to the Curia.

1432 Pope Eugene IV confers prebendary of the Collegiate Church of Santa María de Nieva upon Alfonso Martínez de Toledo.

1433 A deposition of Martínez de Toledo's benefices tells us he was Archpriest of Talavera, one of fifty chaplains of the Chapel of Ancient Kings, prebendary of Santa María de Nieva, and candidate for several canonries in Toledo Cathedral still in dispute. His annual income is eighty pounds sterling. Cardinal Casanova aligns himself with the Ecumenical Council recently convened in Basel. By doing so he incurs the wrath of the Pope and is forced to flee Rome. Alfonso Martínez de Toledo returns to Spain after two years in Italy.

1436 An authorization of sale alludes to Alfonso Martínez de Toledo, chaplain of Juan II. On June 18, in a bull given at Bologna, Eugene IV reinstates Martínez de Toledo to a usurped canonry in the Cathedral of Toledo.

1438 March 15: Martínez de Toledo finishes *Arcipreste de Talavera* (*Archpriest of Talavera*).

1443 Now Royal Chronicler, Martínez de Toledo begins work on his *Atalaya de las crónicas* (*Watchtower of the Chronicles*).

1444 Martínez de Toledo completes his *Vidas de San Ildefonso y San Isidoro* (*Lives of San Ildefonso and San Isidoro*).

1445 *Cancionero de Baena* (*Baena's Songbook*) is completed. Battle of Olmedo, where rebellious nobles suffer severe setback.

1448 August 26: Archpriest purchases Françesc Eiximenis's *Libro de las donas* (*Book of the Ladies*). Also autographs a *Crónica troyana* (*Chronicle of Troy*), and lists his ecclesiastical and university titles.

1453 Don Alvaro de Luna is publicly executed in Valladolid.

1454 Enrique IV succeeds to the throne of Castile after the death of his father, Juan II.

1465 Civil war breaks out in Castile. Don Alonso, Enrique IV's brother, is declared king of Castile by rebellious nobles. He is later poisoned.

1466 Still active in Church affairs, Martínez de Toledo serves as arbiter in a dispute concerning the Hospital of Mercy in Toledo.

1468 January 2: Alfonso Martínez de Toledo dies. In a bull dated March 7, Paul II names Nicolás Fernández the new Archpriest of Talavera de la Reina.

CHAPTER 1

Life and Times of Alfonso Martínez de Toledo

FROM the beginning of the fourteenth century to the middle of the fifteenth, Europe was undergoing one of the most complicated, bewildering, and crucial periods of its history. Fratricidal wars, struggles between nobility and monarchy, church and government, the ruling class and the Third Estate rocked the continent. It was the age of the Great Plagues, the Hundred Years' War, and the Great Schism; of chaos, fear, and superstition. Yet, it was also the age of Petrarch, Boccaccio, Chaucer, Froissart, and Juan Ruiz; of incipient humanism, individualism, and the rise of vernacular literature.

I *The Castilian Political Setting*

At the close of the fourteenth century, Castile had seen little peace in more than five generations. Since the death of Alfonso the Learned in 1284 she had been wracked by seemingly continuous civil war. On the one hand, the power of the monarchy was diminished as a result of the incessant challenges of an increasingly contentious nobility and the succession of children to the throne. On the other hand, the Church could offer no remedy since it was itself tormented by perilous internal strife. By 1369 Enrique de Trastamara had murdered his half-brother, Pedro the Cruel, involved the kingdom in the Hundred Years' War, and brought havoc upon the Jewish population through violent pogroms. His son and successor, Juan I, abortively attempted to unite the Castilian and Portuguese crowns, but was twice defeated by the Portuguese, notably at Aljubarrotta in 1385. Forced to defend his throne against the pretensions of

John of Gaunt, he arranged a marriage between his son, Enrique, and John's daughter (herself a grandchild of Pedro the Cruel) in a gesture of conciliation. The brief and relatively calm reign of Enrique III (1390–1406) proved to be the lull in the storm—the anarchy, dissension, and confusion characterizing the previous decades resurged after his death.

II *Juan II: Politics and Art*

In 1406, at twenty-two months of age, Juan II succeeded to the throne of Castile. The next thirteen years were tumultuous. During his minority, and indeed throughout the remainder of his reign until his death in 1454, the nobility repeatedly attempted to wrest control of the kingdom from the monarchy. History would in the long run prove futile the nobles' efforts to reassert their waning power, but the intensity of their struggle during Juan's reign is significant. Politically, the Middle Ages were coming to an end. In this period we witness their initial death throes and the first signs of life of the coming Renaissance.

Juan II possesses the dubious distinction of being considered Spain's first weak king. Yet it is during his reign that serious attempts to consolidate monarchical power were initiated. Under the brilliant, if unscrupulous, leadership of his favorite, Alvaro de Luna, Constable of Castile, strong and partially successful efforts to liquidate the authority of the nobles were begun. The enlightened don Alvaro was sympathetic to the newly emerging bourgeoisie and champion of international commerce for Castile. His defeat of the nobility at the battle of Olmedo in 1445 represented a milestone (political and social as well as military) in the eventual extinction of the class, and led to the formation of Europe's first modern state.

In consonance with the decline of feudalism, the period also signals the beginning of another transition, one toward a new social and intellectual existence for the nobles. It is the dawn of the age of the prince and courtier. The once powerful warlords were slowly, if unconsciously, being transformed into men of the court. The heroic values of previous generations were evolving into more abstract and often genteel pursuits prefiguring the flowering of humanism in the next century. As

Marcelino Menéndez y Pelayo tells us, "it is no longer the disordered impulse, blind temerity, the quickened pace of the blood, brute strength, the appetite for war or spoils that decide the course of events, but rather the skillful machinations of the intellect, sagacity, and the ability to analyze conditions and the weaknesses of men."[1] The chaotic political climate, then, was accompanied by a changing temperament conducive to intellectual, as well as cultural, achievements.

Juan II, a lover of the arts, provided fertile ground in his court for this emerging humanistic sensibility, and it is there the first echoes of Dante, Petrarch, and Boccaccio are heard in Castilian. Several generations of the aristocratic and courtly poets surrounding the king contributed to a monumental anthology compiled by Juan Alfonso de Baena. The *Cancionero de Baena* (*Baena's Songbook*), ca. 1445, represents a critical turning point in medieval Spanish letters. In it, the provincialism of the early Galician-Portuguese school of poetry is slowly abandoned and replaced by a new cosmopolitan attitude looking directly to Provence and Italy for inspiration. In very general terms, there are two pronounced trends prevailing in Baena's compendium: on the one hand, the Italianate allegorical, philosophical poetry represented by Francisco Imperial and his followers; and on the other, the virtuoso courtly love lyric, rooted in the Provençal tradition, of poets like Alfonso Alvarez de Villasandino and Macías. The poetry of both tendencies, however, is characterized by a new common note—it is perfectionist, elitist, and a pure reflection of the gallant palace atmosphere in which it was created.

At the court of Juan II, prose as well as poetry mirrored the fresh susceptibilities of the ongoing cultural revolution. Boccaccio's *Fiametta* (*Little Flame*) and Aeneas Silvius Piccolomini's *Historia de Duobus Amantibus* (*History of Two Lovers*), both exhibiting courtly attitudes, had begun to circulate in Spain, as had novels of chivalry like the *Amadís de Gaula*. One of the logical outcomes of the popularity of these works was the emergence of the sentimental novel. Juan Rodríguez del Padrón's *Siervo libre de amor* (*Love's Willing Servant*), ca. 1440, Spain's first sentimental novel, projects a quasi-autobiographical event on a poetic, chivalrous, and allegorical background of exacerbated amorous sensibilities. The origins of the modern Spanish essay also stem from this milieu. Alvaro de Luna's *Libro de las virtuosas et claras mujeres* (*Book of Virtuous and Illustrious Women*), patterned after Boccaccio's *De Claris Mulieribus* (*Concerning Illustrious Women*), is an eloquent, urbane, and courtly essayistic defense of femininity. And Fernán Pérez de Guzmán's *Generaciones y semblanzas* (*Generations and Portraits*), comparable to Plutarch's *Lives*, betrays an affinity for classical forms of the historical essay-portrait.

Alongside this cultural zenith, however, the kingdom's political strife and its attendant social and ethical disarray intensified and was itself reflected in certain literary works. Indeed, as early as the mid-fourteenth century, Castilian literature began to express a profound critical pessimism and moral concern. Such extraordinary works as Sem Tob's *Proverbios morales* (*Moral Proverbs*), the anonymous *Libro de la miseria de omne* (*Book of Human Misery*), Pero López de Ayala's *Rimado de palacio* (*Palace Rhymes*), and Juan Ruiz's *Libro de buen amor* (*Book of Good Love*) prefigure the atmosphere of ethical crisis visible in the literature of the coming century.

Literature in the fifteenth century frequently became a vehicle for bitter satire, ironic and often savage polemic. During Juan II's reign, for example, the slanderous and understandably anonymous *Coplas de la panadera* (*Bakerwoman's Couplets*) maliciously bewailed the moral lassitude rampant in the kingdom, cursing and accusing both the pro– and anti–Alvaro de Luna forces taking part in the battle of Olmedo. Social, religious, and political protest even inspired the gallant poets in *Baena's Songbook*. Ferrán Sánchez de Calavera, Ruy Páez de Ribera, and Fernán Manuel de Lando, among others, all had occasion to dip their pens in vitriol.

However, "it is in the time of Enrique IV, Juan II's successor, that the literature of protest reaches its high water mark."[2] The reign of Enrique the Impotent signaled the inspiration for works of a violent, politically subversive, and insistently puritanical attitude: for example, the *Coplas de Mingo Revulgo* (*Couplets of Mingo Commonman*), and the slanderous *Coplas del provincial* (*Provincial's Couplets*). The literary climax of these years of political, social, and moral tumult and disaffection came with the publication of the *Celestina* during the reign of the Catholic Kings.

From early on, then, paralleling the literary gallantries of the court of Juan II, Castilian letters conveyed a pronounced current of complaint. An overriding ethical concern is their prime mover and satire their principal weapon. Satire, as we shall see in our discussion of Alfonso Martínez de Toledo, never exists unto itself: it is a vehicle used to express deep-seated social ferment.

III *The Life of Alfonso Martínez de Toledo*

Alfonso Martínez de Toledo, as a member of Juan II's court, witnessed and contributed to this turbulent and culturally brilliant age. The epigraph to his most famous work, *Arcipreste de Talavera* (*Archpriest of Talavera*), or the so-called *Corbacho* (*Whip*), indicates that he was born in 1398. The inscription reads as follows: "This book was composed by Alfonso Martínez de Toledo, Archpriest of Talavera, at the age of forty years. It was completed on the fifteenth day of March, in the year of our Saviour Jesus Christ, 1438."[3] Precious little more is known about the life of this extraordinary Castilian writer. Cristóbal Pérez Pastor, his first biographer and first modern editor of *Arcipreste de Talavera*, suggests he was a native of Toledo and therefore saw fit to place "de Toledo" ("from Toledo") after his patronym in order to distinguish himself from the many men of his day named Alfonso Martínez. Pérez Pastor convincingly strengthens this argument by revealing a holograph made by our author, an avid bibliophile, in a manuscript of a *Crónica troyana* (*Chronicle of Troy*). In this signature he refers to himself only as "Alfonso Martínez, Archpriest of Talavera, portionary of the Cathedral of Toledo, and hailing from that city."[4] Pérez Pastor reasons that "on the one hand, it seems strange that in an autobiographical note the writer might fail to mention his second last name or complement of the first one; and on the other, it should be noted that 'hailing from,' although not as precise as we might wish, could well be used in the sense of *native* or *citizen* of Toledo."[5] In the explicit of one of his works, *La vida de San Ildefonso* (*Life of San Ildefonso*),

Martínez once again alludes to his place of birth: "Oh, citizen of the imperial heavens, Ildefonso, native of Toledo, pray to Jesus Christ for me, Alfonso, because I was born a sinner where you once reigned."[6] Since San Ildefonso, Archbishop of Toledo, ruled over the city from 657 to 667, the assumption that Alfonso Martínez was indeed born there may be drawn from this note.

The complete epigraph of the *Life of San Ildefonso* and the holograph in the *Chronicle of Troy* also suggest that Martínez de Toledo was university educated. In each of these he refers to himself as a Bachelor at Canon Law. Obviously proud of the title, he later repeats it in the prologue to the *Whip* (11). Pérez Pastor assumes that he attended the University of Salamanca, then one of the most prestigious institutions in Europe. Martín de Riquer, however, a later editor of the *Archpriest of Talavera*, thinks it more likely he took his degree at Toledo, since "by 1415 he was enjoying a benefice ... from the diocese" of this city.[7] However, recent findings by Professor Derek W. Lomax seem to indicate that our author was associated with Salamanca. Nevertheless, Lomax does not gainsay that he could have studied at another, even foreign, university.[8] Whatever the case may be, we may easily believe Martínez's claim that he was academically trained; he possesses one of the most vast vocabularies of any fifteenth-century Castilian writer; and he was thoroughly versed in the ecclesiastical and humanistic literature of his times.

Verardo García Rey, in what remains the most cogent biographical study on Martínez de Toledo, reveals that the young cleric held the title of prebendary in the Chapel of His Grace King Sancho, or of the Ancient Kings, of Toledo Cathedral from 1415 to at least 1418. In a manuscript from the Cathedral Archives, the name of our author appears as the eleventh of the twelve clerics then assigned to the chapel. This is a particularly interesting document. It reveals that "Alfonso Martínez de Toledo was entitled to two hundred fifty *maravedís* from the distributions, and one hundred twenty-nine from the masses: two ducats total."[9] This autograph note, although parenthetical, shows he held an important and reasonably lucrative position for a youth of seventeen. Taking note only of the manuscript's signature (which reads simply "Alfonso Martínez"), and neglecting to cite the text above it, Professor Lomax in his forthcoming study denies that Martínez de Toledo was prebendary in the chapel, preferring to think this holograph belongs to Alfonso Martínez de Burguillos, some years afterward a chaplain of Ancient Kings, as well as treasurer and churchwarden of the cathedral. In later years, however, there were up to as many as fifty chaplains assigned to this chapel, and the 1415 autograph in García Rey's findings must, in the final analysis, speak for itself. It clearly reads "Alfonso Martínez de Toledo."

In his youth our author traveled widely throughout the Iberian Peninsula, spending considerable time in the Crown of Aragon. In the *Whip*, for example, he relates several anecdotes of incidents he claims to have witnessed with his own eyes. One of these took place in Valencia,[10] four in Tortosa (68–70), and another in Barcelona (157–58). Pérez Pastor ventures that the Archpriest was in the Crown of Aragon from approximately 1420 to 1430,[11] since his *Atalaya de las crónicas* (*Watchtower of the Chronicles*), begun in 1443, mentions that he experienced the great earthquakes that shook Catalonia in 1427 and 1428:

> Another time when I was in Barcelona, daily for almost two years, give or take some time, I heard the earth shake as if from down under. It would start almost imperceptibly and later become increasingly louder, bellowing for the time it takes to say a Credo. And finally the great noise would make the entire city, the towers, and all the earth tremble. . . . These and infinite other things happened during that time, which was approximately in the year fourteen hundred twenty. I saw it with my own eyes; and I was in it; and I suffered great fear and tribulation, as did the one hundred thousand, nay, seven hundred thousand people who experienced it, indeed the whole of Catalonia.[12]

Recalling the events some fifteen years after they happened, Martínez is mistaken as to the dates of the great earth tremors. Nevertheless, the confusion is significant, and may indicate that he made more than one trip to Catalonia. In the first place, he clearly recalls being in Barcelona around the year 1420; and in the second, he begins his description with the words "another time when I was in Barcelona," indicating that he visited the city on more than one occasion. It is therefore possible that the quakes experienced during a 1427–1428 sojourn were transposed in memory during later life upon an earlier visit.

If in fact Martínez de Toledo was in Catalonia during the early part of the decade, he had returned to Castile by 1424. In this year, according to Professor Lomax, he began litigation against the canon of Talavera de la Reina, Fernán García, for the archpriestship of the city. The final judgment must have been in Martínez's favor because by 1427 he was in possession of the coveted post (*Bulario*, documents 694, 762). Martínez describes the duties of this office in his *Vida de Sanct Isidoro* (*Life of San Isidoro*), another of his hagiographies: "The archpriest owes obedience to the archdeacon and the bishop. He is responsible for all the priests of the parish and must remain in the church continuously, celebrating the mass and leading the prayers in the absence of the bishop."[13] Moreover, the post required him to head the local church tribunal, hearing litigation and passing judgment on ecclesiastical matters of contention.

According to Pedro de Alcocer's *Hystoria, o descripción de la imperial cibdad de Toledo* (*History, or Description of the Imperial City of Toledo*), one "Alfonso Martínez" is credited with giving a large sum of money toward the construction of the Monastery of Saint Bernard in 1427. Erich von Richthofen's assertion that this is the Archpriest himself is probably a mistake.[14] The cleric mentioned here is most likely Alfonso Martínez de Burguillos, because he is said to be the treasurer and churchwarden of the cathedral. Papal bulls from 1422 and 1424 identify Burguillos as the treasurer (*Bulario*, documents 650, 689, 695, 868)—a position he still held as late as 1433—while in all the documentation now available Martínez de Toledo never once lays claim to the office.

In the days of Alfonso Martínez de Toledo, a cleric named to a benefice was by no means guaranteed the post in perpetuity. In fifteenth-century Castile, as in ensuing centuries, there was heavy and often bitter competition among the clergy for the ranks and offices distributed by the Church. Even after a position was granted to an individual, it was subject to continual challenges by well-connected competitors also seeking its prestige and income. Our author, like countless others, was subjected on more than one occasion to the need to litigate in defense of his titles. In 1427, Francisco Fernández, an ambitious priest from Toledo, wrote Pope Martin V asking for the archpriestship of Talavera de la Reina on the grounds that its current holder, Alfonso Martínez de Toledo, had lost his right to retain it because he was cohabiting with a woman. Commenting upon this recent discovery of his, Derek Lomax suggests that perhaps Martínez had not yet been ordained a priest, hence was not subject to the vows of celibacy and thus was not transgressing eccelesiastical law. However, we have seen Martínez closely associated with the Church since the age of seventeen, and that he was not yet ordained by the age of twenty-nine seems improbable. Moreover, in light of the fact that he was an archpriest at this time, a rank requiring ordination, he surely must have taken his final vows by the time of Fernández's allegation.[15] If we take seriously Francisco Fernández's petition (and indeed we should, for accusations of this nature were not made lightly), we may have encountered at least a partial explanation of our author's oft-cited insights into the female psyche. His experiences living with a woman may well have provided him with much of the raw material for the portraits of feminine wiles he paints in the second part of the *Whip*.

Despite Fernández's zealous protestations to the Pope, Alfonso managed to retain his archpriestship. Perhaps under pressures from his superiors, however, he abandoned the diocese of Toledo, and presumably his lady friend, for a prudent and prolonged visit to Catalonia; the year is 1427, and we find him in Barcelona experiencing the great earthquakes mentioned earlier. With Martínez tactfully "lying low" in the Crown of Aragon, Fernández's petition went unheeded. In 1430, Martínez, with the aid of Cardinal San Sixto (Juan de Casanova), coaxed the promise of a new benefice in the same Cathedral of Toledo from Martin V. The newly pledged title was not easy to secure, however, because in 1431 he was forced to litigate for it with another contender, Domingo González, the deacon of Toledo. The case was slow in coming to judgment, and the inaction of the Spanish ecclesiastical bureaucracy no doubt exasperated Alfonso. To all appearances, he took matters into his own hands and traveled to Rome to present his case in person to the Curia.

Cardinal Casanova's acquaintance, probably initiated during Martínez's 1427–1428 sojourn in Barcelona, proved invaluable to the young cleric. With his help, he continued to accumulate nominations for benefices. In 1432 he obtained one prospectively worth twenty pounds sterling per year (although likely lost to Pedro Gómez, a priest from Cuenca), and he won another in Santa María de Nieva in Segovia, conferred upon him by Pope Eugene IV in December of 1432.

At that time, then, Martínez was reaching the heights of his ecclesiastical career. In a deposition dated February 28, 1433 (*Bulario*, document 864), he lists the titles and benefices he holds or expects to hold: Archpriest of Talavera, chaplain in the Chapel of Ancient Kings (under royal patronage; thus he was favored by the king), the prebendary of the collegiate church of Santa María de Nieva in Segovia, and several canonries in Toledo Cathedral still in litigation. With the exception of the disputed canonries, he reveals he has an annual income of eighty pounds sterling, a rather comfortable sum. His favored status notwithstanding, García Rey notes that in 1434 or 1435, for reasons unmentioned, Martínez and another cleric were deprived of their prebendaries in the Chapel of Ancient Kings. Nevertheless, he was allowed to retain his other benefices and successfully appealed the restoration of the eliminated appointment. On June 18, 1436, in a bull given at Bologna, Eugene IV reinstated the two chaplains in their posts.[16]

Under the aegis of the influential Cardinal San Sixto, Alfonso spent the better part of two years in Italy. In 1433, however, Casanova refused to support the papal monarchy and aligned himself with the rebels of the condemned Ecumenical Council recently convened in Basel. In all likelihood deciding that discretion was the better part of valor, his aspiring Castilian protégé thought it best to leave his protection and return to Spain. The tutelage of the enlightened cardinal, a renowned cognoscente, theologian of some merit, author of various ecclesiological works, and erstwhile university professor, must have proved invaluable to the intellectual formation of the Archpriest, for in his household he was doubtless exposed to the most advanced learning the Roman ambient could offer.

The prospects of a brilliant life in the Roman Curia now

frustrated by political events, Martínez returned home to tend to local ecclesiastical affairs, collect books, and write. Once back in Castile his fortunes continued to rise, at least in part. In an authorization of sale dated 1436, discovered by Lomax, our author is described as "the honorable and discreet gentleman, Alfonso Martínez de Toledo, Bachelor at Canon Law, Canon of Santa María [of Talavera] . . . Archpriest of said town, and Chaplain to our sovereign and of the Chapel of Ancient Kings."[17] Since his return from Italy, then, he had been appointed chaplain to Juan II and had become a member of his court.

What little is known of Alfonso Martínez's life, therefore, seems to indicate that he was a man of influence who continued to advance in the Castilian ecclesiastical and social hierarchy, even after some ostensibly severe setbacks. Although his parentage still remains in question, Lesley Byrd Simpson may be correct in venturing that Alfonso's prominence is the result of his being the natural son of an important prelate.[18] Indeed, in the *Whip* our author reacts strongly to clerical immorality and the stigma of illegitimacy, perhaps recalling some of his personal experiences and unconsciously betraying a clue to his own origins. Psychologically, at least in part, Martínez's antifeminism in the *Whip* might also be a reaction to his illegitimacy —a way of expiating guilt and compensating for feelings of inferiority and personal frustration.

Alfonso Martínez probably spent the latter half of his life at court, ultimately settling down in Toledo during his last years. According to a manuscript cited by Pérez Pastor, he was still active in Church affairs as late as 1466, serving as arbiter in a dispute between the patients and administrators of the Hospital of Mercy in Toledo and the prebendaries of the Chapel of Ancient Kings.[19] Moreover, a later document from the Toledan Capitular Archives of the Guild of Holy Charity reveals he was archdeacon of the city at the time of his death.[20]

From the little evidence available to us (the inscription on a disputed tombstone, a papal bull), it appears probable that Martínez died on January 2, 1468, in his seventieth year.

In a bull dated March 7, 1468, Pope Paul II names Nicolás Fernández to succeed the recently demised Alfonso Martínez de Toledo as Archpriest of Talavera (*Bulario*, document 1218b).

The announcement of the new appointment, allowing enough time for news of the vacancy to reach Rome, suggests that Martínez's death took place at the beginning of that year.

A tombstone purported to mark the grave of Martínez was located in Toledo Cathedral by García Rey in 1928. According to him, the inscription of the stone reads as follows: "Archpriest of Talavera, Toledan, Prebendary, King Sancho's Chaplain, likewise of Enrique IV. MC°CCLX. Died 2 January" (*Archipresbiter Talaveranus, Toletanus, Portionarius, Regis Sancii Capellanus, Itidem Henrici 4, MC°CCLX. Obitidie 2 Henarius*). Although the monument does not specifically name the deceased, it does bear a quartered coat of arms. In the upper left- and right-hand corners of the device there appear single sinople trees on fields of gold synonymous with the Martínez name. The remaining quarters carry a lion rampant with gules on an azure field, to all appearances representing the mother's name. This latter emblem has not been linked to any known families. The titles and benefices of the deceased inscribed on the marker correspond to Alfonso's: Archpriest of Talavera, and prebendary of the cathedral. Moreover, García Rey adduces later testimonials (the *Arcayos* manuscript, ca. 1580, from the archives of the cathedral) identifying the headstone as that of "Alonso Martínez, Archpriest of Talavera, Archdeacon of Toledo, and King Sancho's Chaplain in the Chapel of Ancient Kings."[21] In addition, various documents from the Guild of Holy Charity (dated 1543, 1578, 1636, 1664, and 1772) recall an endowment of one thousand *maravedís*, collectible against the rents of several houses in San Miguel el Alto. These were bequeathed by the Archpriest so that his tomb could be well cared for and masses be said for his soul on All Saint's Day.

Professor Lomax, in his forthcoming article, rejects García Rey's contention that this stone marks Alfonso Martínez de Toledo's final resting place, since the year of demise given in García Rey's hand-drawn reproduction of it reads 1360 in roman numerals. However, in the text of his article the latter quotes the date 1460 throughout. Lomax disregards the fact that the full inscription accurately mentions Martínez's benefices, heraldically alludes to his patronym, and also names Enrique IV, king of Castile from 1454 to 1474. (In fact, it indicates that

Martinez was also chaplain to this monarch.) The year of death on the drawing of the tombstone is probably García Rey's mistake. To make matters more confusing, this is compounded by a mason's error pointed out by García Rey. The marker reads *1460* and not *1468*, as it should. Nevertheless, in light of the bull naming Martínez's successor (dated March 7, 1468), the date of death, January 2, is probably correct. The time elapsed from the beginning of January to the first week in March is just long enough to have prompted papal action. Hence, Alfonso Martínez de Toledo most likely succumbed in Toledo on January 2, 1468.

As evidenced, the available information on our author's life is somewhat confused and at best rather sparse. Nevertheless, future searches as thorough as the one recently undertaken by D. W. Lomax should certainly turn up new and precious material to help us better understand the life and works of the Archpriest of Talavera, Spain's most important prose writer of the first half of the fifteenth century.

CHAPTER 2

General Considerations on the Archpriest of Talavera *or the* Whip

I *Genre and Content*

ALFONSO Martínez de Toledo chose to name his most famous work after himself: that is, after one of his ecclesiastical titles. In the epigraph to the book he demands that the treatise, "without the benefit of baptism . . . be called whithersoever it may be borne, the *Archpriest of Talavera*" (9). We shall return to this matter in a later chapter, but before any conclusions on the title's origins or significance may be drawn, an examination of the work's content, text, and critical fortunes is necessary.

The *Archpriest of Talavera* belongs, according to Anna Krause, "to that loosely defined literary genre known as the *tractado* [tractate] . . . an outgrowth of the *tractatus* used by the Church Fathers to expound classical knowledge under the guidance of medieval religious standards."[1] Resembling the essay, then, the treatise has no plot to speak of, but does make use of exempla (short, illustrative, moralizing anecdotes with their own internal story line) to simplify the author's thesis. Many of these comic, vernacular, and often grotesque, episodes are derived from the wealth of the medieval preaching tradition, while others are totally original with the Archpriest. A primary source for them, he tells us, is his own life, since experience is the only true reformer. Indeed, adopting a posture of the worldly-wise teacher, he warns that his book contains no fiction:

Do not think that he who writes this speaks merely from hearsay, for he witnessed much of it. . . . Reading about such things is profitable, to be sure, and understanding them is a help, but practice and experience are the best teachers of everything. . . . What one man went through, with many hardships and dangers and suffering, and what he saw with his own person and wrote down on a piece of paper, let this teach others and serve as a lesson against evil-doing, a remedy for wickedness, and a warning against the pitfalls of this world. (96–97)

The book's unity is derived from this autobiographical point of view, and its thematic organization centers on the condemnation of the sin of lust. A satirico-didactic work divided into four parts, it examines and reproves certain amatory beliefs and conventions present in fifteenth-century Castilian society.

A long sermonic *ars amatoria* (art of loving) entitled "On the reprobation of mad love," Part I consists of thirty-eight short chapters adducing the spiritual and physical dangers of concupiscence. In them, Martínez reveals how lust underlies most of human amorous behavior, and thus is the fountainhead of all evil. He also shows how lust, transgressing His every moral and religious law, is contrary to the will of God. He proves, for example, how one by one the Ten Commandments are broken by uncontrollable passion, and how the attainment of virtue is all but impossible in the pursuit of worldly love. The lustful lover courts disaster, he tells us, because his appetite invariably leads him to commit all seven of the deadly sins. The only true, righteous path leading to salvation, he concludes, is through the infinite, unquestioned love of the Creator.

The second part, consisting of fourteen chapters, deals with "the vices, blemishes, and evil ways of wicked and vicious women, applauding the virtuous in their virtues" (99). Despite this declaration of intent, however, virtuous women are few and far between. Part II is perhaps the best-known section of the work, for in it are found the raucous, often bawdy, graphic exempla picturing feminine foibles. Adopting an unmistakably misogynistic attitude, notwithstanding his intention to applaud certain meritorious ladies, Martínez intimates that woman is the sole instrument of man's perdition. Shrewdly avoiding passing direct judgment upon her, he permits her to portray herself in his dramatic anecdotes. In hilarious, earsplitting dialogues and monologues, woman shows herself to be what the Archpriest thinks she is: avaricious, envious, voluble, disobedient, scatterbrained, vain, sniveling, and lustful. The following tirade, depicting a woman jealous of another more beautiful than she, is just one of many examples of his antifeminism:

Is she the only beautiful woman you've ever seen? Well, really! God help us! Indeed! What's the matter with you? Oho, what a miracle! As if we had never seen her equal! What a lot of wonders you've seen and miracles that don't amount to a row of pins! Oh, she's beautiful enough. A woman is certainly beautiful if she's got a good figure, but I know a thing or two about that, and I'll say no more. If I only dared to speak. . . . Well, I will speak, because I'd burst if I didn't, by God! I saw her the other day, this one you think is so beautiful and praise so much, I saw her talking to an abbot, and giggling and frolicking with him in his house, and pinching him and sticking him with pins, and shrieking with laughter: Upon my word, that's what I saw, and I won't say another word, because the abbot's red face didn't come from saying matins, nor did hers from spinning at her wheel! God's wrath! Good women would not be seen among those scoundrels, by God! The devil take such goings-on! How many poor wretches of men do such wicked women snare with their paint and powder! (120–21)

Most women are wicked, Martínez contends, but he does portray a few (usually repentant sinners, or those who have been sexually exploited) as the victims of the world's evil ways.

In what appears to be a halfhearted attempt to counter his censorious antifeminism, the Archpriest ends his discourse on women and prepares us for Part III with the following:

Since the purpose of this book is the reprobation of worldly love and praise of the love of God, and since up to this point I have reproved the love of women, it would not be fitting for me to praise the love of men. If women wish to love men, let them consider who it is they love, what profit there is in it, and what virtues and vices men have for loving. And since men are not commonly reproved in this as women are—this because of their greater sense and judgement[!]—it will be fitting, then, to speak of each man according to his nature, which cannot be known without the natural science of the astrologers. (164)

Dealing with "the various complexions of men: what they are and what virtues such men have for loving and being loved" (12), the ten chapters of Part III form a small treatise on iatromathematia, or the pseudo-scientific synthesis of astrology and medicine. Based on the medieval interpretations of Galen (often confused by the medieval mind with Hippocrates), it divides men into four temperaments—phlegmatic, sanguine, choleric, and melancholic—relating these to their corresponding signs of the zodiac so as to determine each type's predisposition for love. The sanguine man, inevitably a Gemini, Aquarius, or Libra, is potentially pleasure-loving and happy. On the other hand, the choleric, an Aries, Leo, or Sagittarius, is prone to violence and fury. The phlegmatic, a Cancer, Scorpio, or Pisces, tends to be sour-tempered; and finally, the melancholic, either a Taurus, Virgo, or Capricorn, is usually sad and gloomy.

The men in Part III, however, prove clearly less attractive targets than the women; but just the same they do incur some criticism. Perhaps recalling his own days as a Lothario, the reformed Archpriest, for example, censures the choleric's indiscretions which forced him to flee his native land—all, of course, on account of the frivolous, sniveling mistress who taunted him into killing a man in order to avenge a trifling insult:

> He will lose his possessions and live in hiding and run away, abandoning his country and his house, and will wander about in foreign parts, making a living for magistrates, constables, and notaries, and all because of those accursed, damned, unlucky, poisonous, cruel, and monstrous tears! O Lord, would that I could weigh the tears of a woman, had I but the knowledge! Truly, a single tear of hers outweighs a hundred weight of lead or copper! A curse upon him, amen, who does not ponder this and who, when he sees a woman in tears, does not consider that they are merely an instrument of vengeance on the part of the one who lacks discretion, sense, and understanding. (184–85)

Although man is righteously punished for his sometimes venial lack of better judgment, the true cause of his tribulations is attributed to woman. While ostensibly censuring men in Part III, the Archpriest has trouble masking his resolute contempt for women. For example, if the innate gaiety of the sanguine man may lead him to lechery, the fault usually lies as much with the object of attraction as with the sinner. If the melancholy man is prone to quarreling, the last straw is usually heaped upon him by a feminine hand. And finally, if the phlegmatic man is a sometimes cowardly and slothful wretch, he is even more so because his ladylove demands too much. Disgusted with him, she invariably hurls "an abundance of curses, insults unnumbered, figs, snorts, and whistles like those of an ox driver, and she says: 'May your mother enjoy you'" (189) to the now doubly careworn male victim.

In Parts I, II, and III, despite his continuous criticism of her, Martínez occasionally declares himself woman's advocate. Yet he never truly attempts to picture her as other than the double-edged sword of mad love: either as the tantalizing object, or as Providence's instrument of vengeance. He was of course aware of his misogynistic tone, for he frequently, although unconvincingly, attempts to check his high-spirited elucidation of feminine wiles by affirming man's similar depravity. These modifications, however, usually take the form of an afterthought and smack of formulaic mitigation: "You will see widows as well as wives take up with base, ugly, poor, luckless, and worthless men, crippled, one-armed or one-eyed, and even hunchbacks. And I say no more. When women love men of this kind they do so for two reasons. The first is that they are like bitch wolves, for cold and love cannot be kept out, and they get heated over the first one who happens by and would go to bed with him. Men do the same" (55).

The fourth and last section of the *Archpriest of Talavera*, curiously referred to as "the middle part of this book and work," reproves in three long chapters "the vulgar error of those who believe in fate, luck, fortune, signs, and planets" in order to "correct those who say that if they have sinned in love, their fate or fortune made them do so" (12). A long, elegant, scholastic essay qualifying the astrobiological beliefs and their relation to loving expounded in Part III, it is an emphatic affirmation of the Christian dogma of free will.

While previously allowing for the use of the horoscope in determining what sort of temperament a man may possess, in

Part IV Martínez attacks judicial astrology; that is to say, the belief that the position of the stars at an individual's birth can foretell specific events in his life—whether, for example, he will be a good lover or a mad lover, righteous or evil, a success or a failure. The stars, he concludes, may indeed determine a man's physical makeup, but never his moral fiber. They may predispose him to certain forms of amatory behavior, as he shows in Part III, but never fully cause it. Hence we are all responsible for our actions, and must use our reason, intellect, and will in avoiding sin and eternal damnation. Wicked, worldly lovers are what they are not because of fate or the stars, but because they have become lustful by their own volition. Of course, this thesis of accountability is central to Christian theology, for without it there could be no sin.

As in the previous three parts of the work, Martínez illustrates his exposition with comical and often ironic exempla. In this section, however, the anecdotes are lengthier and sometimes, as in the case of the Valencian hermit's tale, approach being fully developed short stories, squarely exploring the literary problems of time, space, narrator, character, and plot.

II *The Text*

As of this writing, a critical edition of the *Archpriest of Talavera* has not yet been completed, and the single manuscript and three incunabala pose some important textual problems. Sections of the prologue and Part I constitute, as remains to be shown, a long sermon against lust. Parts II and III, as Erich von Richthofen points out, are stylistically and structurally very different from Part I.[2] In our mind, these disparities point to the possibility that the work might have originated as a homily condemning cupidity and later been elaborated to form a lengthy treatise on the theme of love. That is, Part I was probably originally intended as a sermon and later expanded, added to, in order to create an extensive prose commentary on the evils of worldly love and women. Furthermore, the end of Part III, which reads "here ends the third part of this book and work" (197), as Mario Penna observes, "has all the indications of an explicit,"[3] suggesting in all likelihood Part IV was written at a later date, or that it reflects a different manuscript tradition. The fact that the last section bears the rubric "middle part" (*media parte*) would seem to support this conclusion.

The earliest extant manuscript of Martínez's treatise is codex h. III. 10 of the Escurial Library. It is commonly referred to as the Contreras manuscript, after Alfonso de Contreras, the scribe who copied it in 1466.[4] At one time it belonged to Queen Isabella of Castile, although because of its crude binding Mario Penna doubts it was ever intended for her perusal.[5] Since it is the earliest known copy of the work, the Contreras codex has been, in the main, the basis for all modern editions of the *Archpriest of Talavera.*

Apart from this earliest known manuscript, three incunabula of the *Archpriest of Talavera* have come down to us. A fourth is described by Francisco Escudero y Perosso in his *Tipografía hispalense*, but Konrad Haebler, describing the 1498 Seville edition, comments that "following Panzer, Escudero cites an edition from 1495. However, what Panzer says is taken from Diosdado Caballero (Additions) and hence merits little confidence. I believe the 1498 edition is the first."[6] Thus, to all appearances, the Seville 1498 incunabulum is the princeps of the *Archpriest of Talavera.* The second incunabulum (Toledo, 1499) consists of only Part II of the work and fails to cite the author's name. An edition of the complete work, the third and last incunabulum, was printed in Toledo on July 20, 1500, and its title and explicit correspond identically to those of the 1498 Seville incunabulum.[7]

Between the Contreras manuscript and the two complete incunabula there is a difference of four hundred forty-seven lines. Mario Penna suggests this might be due to the fact that "the editor [of the first incunabulum] altered the text, and was later followed by subsequent editors."[8] On the other hand, von Richthofen believes that the changes and emendations appearing in the printed editions could very well be the work of Alfonso Martínez; that is, corrections made by the Archpriest in later life.[9] The two most important additions consist of a variant of exemplum XIV, "De Puteo" ("Concerning the Well"), of Peter Alphonsus's *Disciplina Clericalis* (*Clerical Instruction*), and an epilogue (*demanda*).

The variant of the "well" exemplum appears in Part II, Chapter 1, of the incunabula. According to von Richthofen, although its style varies from the rest of the work, the anecdote was added by the author sometime after 1438.[10] Penna, on the other hand, persuasively argues that the interpolation seems thematically, as well as stylistically, out of place. While Chapter 1 concerns itself with feminine avarice, the appended well story deals with woman's mendacity.[11] It is therefore unlikely that Martínez, a writer conscious of the structure of his work as his prologue indicates, inserted this anecdote. The difference in style may indeed, as suggested by von Richthofen, be caused by its being a later addition to the text; its unharmonious theme, however, casts serious doubt upon its authenticity.

The epilogue in the incunabula is of far greater importance and complexity than the well story, posing problems that go to the marrow of the work itself. A palinode ostensibly rejecting the tyrannical domination of man by woman as portrayed throughout the four parts of the work, it depicts the author's dream of being attacked by a crowd of irate females who force him to implore forgiveness for his misogyny. By not commenting upon it, Puymaigre and several early scholars seem to tacitly accept its authenticity.[12] However, later critics (Martín de Riquer, Mario Penna, and most especially Christine J. Whitbourn) express doubt that it is from the Archpriest's pen. Arguing in favor of its exclusion, Whitbourn believes that "it would constitute a complete denial of everything Martínez has been at pains to establish in the rest of the work."[13]

We believe, however, that the matter is very subtle indeed, and that the first impression usually evoked by the passage may contain implications not yet fathomed by its critics. As Miss Whitbourn herself points out, stylistically the epilogue shares many common characteristics with the rest of the *Whip*: frequent use of exclamations; colloquial speech; and forms of familiar address directed at the reader. Moreover, the description of the choking, groveling author with a woman's foot at his throat strongly recalls Poverty's abuse of Fortune in Part IV of the work; while the reminder of the narrator's youthful militancy in the service of woman, intoned by a chorus of more than a thousand ladies, might betray an allusion to Martínez's own peccadilloes committed in his salad days.[14] Despite these analogies, however, there are some differences: the tone is sportive and gallant, and the writer mockingly uses religious terminology, referring to successful lovers as "brothers in Jesus Christ" (*Hermanos en Jesuxpo*). What is more, the image of the ludicrous courtly lover so painstakingly outlined throughout the *Archpriest of Talavera* is patently absent.[15] Nevertheless, when examined in the light of contemporary amatory literature, the epilogue contains nothing truly at odds with Martínez's intended lesson.

Von Richthofen declares the palinode authentic, suggesting that it might have been written by Martínez after the completion of the Contreras codex, or perhaps earlier (forming part of a different manuscript tradition), in order to stem attacks against the book's antifeminism.[16] Indeed, similar strategies are common in fifteenth-century misogynistic literature. The courtly woman-haters Pere Torroellas and Juan de Tapia, for example, both wrote bitterly antifeministic poems which they later felt forced to retract.[17] However, their recantations, like, perhaps, the epilogue to the *Whip*, may be looked at as ironic, containing much more than what immediately meets the eye. Insisting upon the last laugh, under the guise of repentance they ingeniously continue to imply woman's evil tyranny over man. Torroellas's so-called retraction, for instance, merely states that he never denigrated women, thereby implying that his first poem, the "Maldezir de mugeres" ("Diatribe Against Women"), was not slanderous but true.[18] Irony seems the key to its interpretation. Similarly, in the epilogue to the *Archpriest of Talavera*, the gentle ladies conquer and force the narrator to admit his error, but not without first having resorted to verbal abuse, terror, and physical violence to extract his confession—the very things they are insistently rebuked for in the body of the work. Perhaps placating his less astute critics through an extorted palinode and a feminine Pyrrhic victory, then, the Archpriest might still ironically be suggesting in the epilogue the lesson of woman's menacing nature. Martínez's thesis would continue to stand, even if it were at the expense of a personal "humiliation." With a malicious twinkle in his eye, he could well have sacrificed himself to the enemy in order to show the error of their ways. The careful reader's sympathies would then go out to the terrorized victim and his "brothers in Jesus Christ," that is to say, fellow martyrs enslaved in the service of love and woman. If looked at from this perspective, there would be no apparent contradiction between the epilogue and the main body of the work.

III *The* Archpriest of Talavera: *Early Detractors, Later Admirers*

The *Archpriest of Talavera* is known to have provoked a chord of indignation from doña María, Juan II's queen.[19] Reproaching the work for its antifeminism (perhaps prompting the addition of the equivocal epilogue), she called for a literary defense of woman which likely stoked the fires of a great debate in fifteenth-century Castilian literature—a phenomenon we will return to in a later chapter. The strong-willed queen is, then, the first critic on record to have judged the merits and condemned the misogyny of the work. During the Renaissance it doubtless also continued to generate a considerable amount of polemical and literary interest, for apart from the incunabula, four sixteenth-century editions of the *Whip* were printed. Indeed, these must have circulated freely, because halfway through the century Juan Justiniano mentions Martínez de Toledo in his preface to the Spanish translation of Luis Vives's *De Institutione Feminae Christianae* (*On the Instruction of Christian Women*). He places the Archpriest among the detractors of woman who have criticized her mercilessly without attempting to provide a remedy for her faults. Despite the fact that he is denounced in this prologue, however, our author is mentioned in the company of some of the most well-known writers of antiquity and the Middle Ages accused by Justiniano of the same sin: Euripides, Boccaccio, and Poggio Bracciolini, among others.[20] Later, Juan de la Cueva, in his drama *El infamador* (*The Defamer*), ca. 1581, publicly took Martínez to task for his notorious malignment of women. In Act III, Scene 2, Porcero asks Eliodora what she has been doing in his absence. Answering that she is melancholy because she spent her time reading the *Archpriest of Talavera,* Porcero is angered and says:

If this is his only fruit,
would that this priest were never born . . .
How much better it would have been
had the reverend Archpriest
remained teaching the parishioners of Talavera . . .
rather than composing this scourge
and offending women.

(*Nunca tal preste naciera*
si no dió más fruto quéste . . .
¡Cuánto mejor le estuviera
al reverendo arcipreste
que componer esta peste
doctrinar a Talavera . . .
que con libertad tan necia
las mujeres ofender!)[21]

A comic censure such as this could not have been made unless Cueva's late-sixteenth-century audience was very familiar with Martínez's work. The *Archpriest of Talavera* was, then, still a widely known book capable of provoking controversial opinions nearly one hundred fifty years after being written. It was alive and well, and in the minds of the Spanish literary public of the Renaissance it continued to exist as one of the important, albeit factious, contributions of their medieval heritage. Later, however, it appears to have fallen into relative obscurity, receiving only brief mention in the eighteenth century as a bibliographical curiosity.[22]

Although it caused an early stir by its antifeminism, it was not until 1850 that Martínez's important artistic contribution to Spanish letters became critically recognized. In that year, the German philologist Ferdinand Wolf published an article in the *Blättern für litterarische Unterhaltung* describing the several editions of the *Archpriest of Talavera* and giving a brief summary of its content, while indicating the parts he deemed of greatest literary and historical importance. Five years after its rediscovery by Wolf, Ludwig Lemcke saw fit to give the work an honored place in his *Handbuch der spanischen Literatur* (*Handbook of Spanish Literature*). Publishing excerpts from it, while insisting on calling it the *Whip*, Lemcke reaffirmed

Martínez's literary importance and heaped praise upon his use of colloquial language. Moreover, he called for a modern edition of the work so that it might be enjoyed more widely.[23]

The first modern Spaniard to take critical notice of Martínez de Toledo was José Amador de los Ríos. In his *Historia crítica de la literatura española* (*Critical History of Spanish Literature*) he discusses the *Archpriest of Talavera* at length, suggesting some of its possible sources and pointing out the work's invaluable wealth of material chronicling the manners and customs of fifteenth-century Castilian society. Noting how Martínez's prose differs radically from that of his contemporaries, he lauds the fluid style of his exempla and his unique use of the vernacular, concluding that because of this, the work continues to be of intense interest and great literary transcendence.[24]

Some years later, the *Archpriest of Talavera* was raised to the justly deserved status of a classic in Marcelino Menéndez y Pelayo's seminal *Orígenes de la novela* (*Origins of the Novel*). This critic perceived Martínez de Toledo as the first Spanish author "to eschew abstractions and arid moralizing, while lending a new vitality to the clichés of medieval didacticism through picturesque, concrete observations of the everyday, and an overflowing treasure trove of popular diction." He goes on to note how it is the first Castilian prose work to make use of the familiar, conversational speech of the plazas and marketplaces, and hence a forerunner of literary realism, concluding that "the *Archpriest of Talavera* opened the door of a new artistic form and, in doing so, buried the symbolic didacticism of previous ages."[25]

Since Menéndez y Pelayo, critics have agreed that the *Whip* represents a fundamental turning point in the development of Spanish prose. And indeed, it is a remarkable work, not only for its shrewd, humorous observations of human folly, but principally because it does represent, in the words of Lesley Byrd Simpson, the "discovery of the limitless possibilities of the vernacular."[26] Without Martínez de Toledo's example to signal the way, the unrestrained facility of Spanish Renaissance and Baroque narrative might never have reached the heights it did. The lively, strident bawdiness of the characters in the *Whip*'s dramatic exempla, its delight in picturing social customs with vivid irony, and its insistence upon an underlying moral order, in more than one way prefigure the picaresque of the *Guzmán de Alfarache* and the novel of Cervantes. On the other hand, the author's elegant, Italianate discourses on ethics and theology, filled with prosodic periods and hyperbaton, announce the future direction of much of the ascetic literature in the Golden Age.

CHAPTER 3

Tradition and Innovation: The Sources of the Archpriest of Talavera

THE principal sources of the *Archpriest of Talavera* have been identified through the diligence of Erich von Richthofen.[1] However, the work's literary importance lies, not in its cultivated and folkloric antecedents, but almost exclusively in the original tone, style, and artistry of Alfonso Martínez de Toledo. For over thirty years the German scholar's erudite study has been considered the definitive statement on the *Whip*, rather than, as it should be, the learned basis upon which new investigations may be carried out. Von Richthofen thoroughly established the intellectual and artistic inheritance of the *Archpriest of Talavera*, cogently describing its place in the didactic literary tradition of the Middle Ages. Nevertheless, as Pedro Salinas wisely points out, "a tradition presents the most complete form of liberty to the writer. His material, the masterpieces of the past, offers the man a plurality of spiritual attitudes, procedures of objectification, triumphs over the inanimate, and methods leading to the realization of his own work. All this is generously bestowed upon him by the past. Creative freedom in a vacuum is worthless. The artist who manages to dominate, come to grips with, a tradition is potentially freer than others because, seeing what has come before him, he searches for new directions of expression."[2] Up until now, the *Archpriest of Talavera* has not been carefully looked at in the light of its author's original contribution to his literary tradition. In this chapter, therefore, we will survey the work's sources and attempt also to pinpoint Alfonso Martínez's own creative exploitation of them.

I Corbacho, Corbaccio, *Boccaccio*

The *Archpriest of Talavera*, somewhere between the time of its completion in 1438 and its first printed edition (1498), acquired the popular title *Corbacho* (*Whip*). This occurred probably through association with Giovanni Boccaccio's misogynistic allegory, *Il Corbaccio* (*The Wicked Crow*). However, the *Whip*'s relation to this work ends with its title and its antifeministic, satirical theme. Although Arturo Farinelli sees a similarity between the Spanish *Corbacho* and the Italian work,[3] a true textual, structural, or stylistic interdependence is untenable.

The *Archpriest of Talavera*'s presumed association with *Il Corbaccio* was probably generated unwittingly by Alfonso Martínez himself, for in Part II, Chapter 3, of his work he presents a long and often quoted imprecation against woman's deceitful and excessive use of cosmetics. Following a detailed, ironic, torrential enumeration of the preparations, ointments, and methods, "she uses to soften and clean her face," he parenthetically notes that "even John Boccaccio writes of the way women deck themselves out . . . though not for long" (115). Possibly through this allusion to the Italian humanist, the *Archpriest of Talavera* became popularly known as the *Corbacho*. As Farinelli states, "*Il Corbaccio* was Boccaccio's most well-known vernacular work in the Middle Ages."[4] When Martínez's work appeared more than eighty years after Boccaccio's, readers of the manuscripts might naturally have associated the Spanish treatise, full of antifeminist vignettes, with the earlier Italian composition, and in their minds identified it as another *Corbaccio*: hence the reason why the hispanified version of the Italian name has been applied to the Archpriest's tract ever since.[5]

Erich von Richthofen's analysis of Martínez's sources proves that Boccaccio was indeed the inspiration for the condemnation of cosmetics in the *Whip*. However, our author's source was not Boccaccio's *Wicked Crow*, as Farinelli presumes, but rather his *De Casibus Virorum Illustrium* (*On the Fates of Illustrious Men*). This is an important didactic treatise of exempla drawn from antiquity and directed against the spiritual decadence of Florence in the 1350s.[6] It is in Book I, Chapter 18, "Against Women" (*In Mulieres*), of the *Fates of Illustrious Men* that the Archpriest found the model for his diatribe against makeup. Although space does not permit a detailed comparison of the two passages, when parts of the one are confronted with the other it becomes evident that Martínez made use of Boccaccio's text, but merely as a source of information. In the *Fates of Illustrious Men*, for example, the narration is severe, direct, and admonitory. It is the worldly-wise Boccaccio who is reproaching woman's vanity and license:

What swollen hands, pimply faces, rheumy eyes, or defects in other parts I could enumerate which have all been cured without calling in the learned Hippocrates? From the same source women obtain waters to make black hair golden, curling irons to make straight hair ringed and wavy; *they make their forehead higher by pulling out their hairs; eyebrows that are too big and joined together, they separate with pincers making the arc less thin. Any teeth which by chance have fallen out, they replace with ivory. What hair they cannot remove from their face with a razor, they remove with nitre,* and they scrape away skin that is too thick. By these techniques they remake themselves so that if you thought before they were unattractive and shapeless, now you will think them Venus herself. Need I mention *the flowers, garlands, fillets, or coronets decked with gold and gems* they decorate themselves with? It is as if they took off their clothes and dressed themselves in a little of the thinnest gold. How can I describe these clothes? These are robes glittering with gold and precious stones fit only for a king. This woman dresses herself like the Narbonnese, that one like one from the Côte d'Or, this one like the *Cyprians*, others like the *Egyptians*, Greeks, or even the *Arabs*. It is no longer sufficient to be dressed like an Italian. [Emphasis added.][7]

Martínez de Toledo, while including much of the information in Boccaccio's reproach, creates a more complex literary portrait. Imposing a narrative distance on the material, he creates a feminine character full of psychological misgivings who reacts with envy to a neighbor's beautiful wife. Fulminating with rage and jealousy, her stubborn pettiness is humorously, yet effectively, demonstrated in her denunciation of the other woman's overdose of cosmetics:

The shameless, slovenly slattern! She can't do fancy work or sew, except with coarse stitches. She can pin, but not fine. She's good for nothing but the bed! . . . She's black as an eclipse! She's as white as my luck was the day I was born! Upon my word, she smears whiting up to her very eyes, and paint, no end! *Her eyebrows well plucked, high and arched,* her eyes darkened with kohl, *her face peeled of its long and short hairs with a mixture of turpentine and oil of camomile*; her lips a bright red, not naturally, of course, but stained with fumitory seeds mixed with brazil wood and alum; *her teeth "anosegados" or scrubbed with "manbre,"* the herb they call Indian; her nails tinted with henna, longer than the claws of a hawk or a falcon, so long that *she has to wear gold braces on them*; her face shining like a sword with all those washes I spoke of. She applies packs to her face, one after the other, for ten days running, because when she doesn't she's as black as a *Moor of the Indies*. She makes them with an ointment of the juice of radish leaves, sugar, and *Cyprian* soap, oil of almonds and French beans cooked with cow's gall. [Emphasis added.] (117–18)

Through the woman's direct speech, then, elements of Boccaccio's exposition are magically converted by the Archpriest into a profound exercise in literary characterization full of dramatic irony. The woman in our author's anecdote is allowed to unleash her self-righteous contempt, in reality inspired by seething envy, upon her unsuspecting neighbor, but not before she has thoroughly convinced the reader of her own niggardly personality.

Although Martínez's tremendous ability to innovate is clearly demonstrated by the only partial comparison we have made, elsewhere in his work he virtually translates Boccaccio directly. He evidently felt free to copy or modify his sources at will. Such borrowings were not uncommon in the Middle Ages. Authors were not obsessed by the concept of originality, as were post-Renaissance writers. Indeed, a formal artistic precedent upon which one's efforts were based was desirable and recommended by some medieval preceptists.[8] In his work, the Archpriest makes no attempt to conceal the sources of his material. For example, he openly introduces his battle of Poverty and Fortune, another episode borrowed from the *Fates of Illustrious Men* (Book III, Chapter 1), with the words, "I will tell you another story, this one from John Boccaccio. It goes like this. . . ."[9]

However, to judge Alfonso Martínez de Toledo a simple imitator is to gravely misconstrue the nature of his art. The key to understanding the esthetics of the *Archpriest of Talavera* is the realization that the work's importance lies not so much in what is said but in how it is said. Through textual comparison with Boccaccio it becomes evident that Martínez's masterful style alone is a valid criterion for his artistry. The Latin narrative is terse, flat, and uninteresting when pitted against the Archpriest's exuberant version of the same episode. Indeed, Boccaccio's allegory of Poverty and Fortune serves only as a point of departure for the creative genius of our author.

A short passage from the episode in the *Fates of Illustrious Men* succinctly tells us that "Poverty was seated at a crossroad dressed in patched clothing, her eyes lowered, as was her custom, for she was turning over many things in her mind" (68). This single sentence is cleverly transformed by Martínez into a detailed, imaginative, novelistic description—a virtual character vignette. The sparse Latin is infused with new life, for in the Spanish text Poverty becomes the dynamic image of a disconsolate beggarwoman who is "very sad and worn, overworked, pensive, aching and emaciated, only skin and bones. Her complexion, black, mangy; her eyes downcast, she ceaselessly scratches her scabies, her flesh pickled and wrinkled, gnashing her teeth—a horrifying beastie" (GM, 252). The same is true of Fortune, whose "well-filled, soft, and sanguine" skin and "rich clothes" (*Fates*, 68) are metamorphosed by the Archpriest into a figure recalling the richly adorned late Gothic "international style" of painting (Broederlam, the Limbourg Brothers, etc.). Coming down the road, she is described by our author as "extremely powerful, thirty years of age, vigorous and courageous, laughing and singing, and with great joy and self-satisfaction mounted upon a hefty, beautiful horse. A garland in her hair, girdled and freshly attired according to the latest fashions" (GM, 252). Martínez's Fortune is every bit the image of youthful prosperity and haughty self-confidence.

The Archpriest is clearly no servile imitator, for between the two works there is a manifest stylistic and creative difference. The Latin source is a simple documentary exposition concerned more directly with ethics and theology than with art.

In contrast, Martínez seems to forget the immediacy of doctrine, happily abandoning himself to the task of creating a narrative that is a sumptuously colored, forceful, personal, and an altogether ingenious characterization of people, not allegorical puppets. His characters are pulsating with vitality. They illustrate and embody the concepts of poverty and fortune as individuals with diverse concerns, while in Boccaccio they remain abstract principles in human dress. Through Martínez de Toledo the Italian's impersonal figures become living beings closely associated to the author's and his readers' immediate experience: a grubby, snorting, diseased beggar; a glib, willful, pompous, and overelegant noblewoman. Selecting, intensifying, analyzing, and imagining lifelike detail, he creates a reality through literary illusion far surpassing the artistic complexity of his model.

Another somewhat static passage in the *Fates of Illustrious Men* describes Fortune coming to blows with Poverty:

Fortune ran at Poverty, waving her arms as if she would pound her into the center of the earth. But Poverty was ready and blocked Fortune with her elbows. Then she spun Fortune around in the air and finally threw her to the ground. Then Poverty pushed her knee into Fortune's chest and pressed her other foot into her neck. Fortune struggled for breath, but Poverty did not permit her to get up until she confessed herself beaten and until she swore an oath that she would faithfully observe the conditions agreed upon before the fight. Victorious Poverty got up and allowed herself some rest, for she was somewhat tired and exhausted. (*Fates*, 70–71)

As before, this is taken by Martínez as the framework for a long, much more dynamic and plastic version of his own, leading one critic to believe he might have been a wrestler since he displays such an intimate knowledge of the sport.[10] Movement, metaphor, sound, dialogue, and colloquial direct speech are our author's dominant contributions to the scene—a scene he expands to nearly six times its original length:

Haughtily, Fortune dismounted her horse. Leaving the reins to fall to the ground she came at Poverty with large, measured steps as would a giant. Although neatly attired, she approached Poverty moving and gesticulating in the manner of a wrestler; alternately hunging her body, rising on her toes, wiggling her shoulders, stretching like a cat, roaring like a lion, her eyes scarlet with anger, gritting her teeth, wanting to scare Poverty off. But Poverty saw through her, thinking all the while: "Fortune, I know your tricks, and you can't frighten me with your fierce gestures in the manner of Italians, Genovese, and Lombards. There's no honor amongst thieves. This can only be settled by coming to blows . . . I know you." Fortune and Poverty came to grips and circled around looking for opportune holds. . . . Bones began to crackle like nuts in a sack. . . . Poverty became frustrated and angry, saying to herself: "This peasant is as heavy as an ox" . . . Suddenly she tried the "old broadside" and Fortune toppled over, her legs flailing in the air, head on the ground. Lifting and spinning her, Poverty crashed her to the ground with such fierceness that Fortune all but burst. Then jumping on top of her with one foot to the throat, practically choking her, Poverty struck Fortune again and again until her eyes were no longer visible from the swelling. All the while saying: "Out, out, damned beauty! You'll no longer exist here anymore! . . ." Finally, Fortune, penitent, exhausted, hands clasped, and naked as the day she was born, with head bowed and eyes downcast, tame and humble, knelt there while Poverty sat triumphant on a nearby fence. . . . Then Poverty took Fortune and tied her securely with chains to a great post stuck in the earth in order that she might never escape (something she has yet to do). This done, Poverty headed toward Bologna, and from there she left to wander over the world—which she still does to this very day. (GM, 263–71)

While Boccaccio's episode is deadly serious, exemplary, indeed an arid medieval allegory, the Archpriest's version takes on satirical overtones through exaggeration and overstatement. In Martínez, we see the medieval mind giving way to art as pure enjoyment. His version not only quantitatively but qualitatively overwhelms its sources with dramatic power, human insight, and plastic detail. Boccaccio's schematic figures are brought to life through action. Infused with psychological realism and an overpowering sense of willful dynamism, their every movement and hesitation is chronicled for the reader. Our author registers Poverty's reticence in a crude, though nevertheless novelistic, free indirect style. Even as the flurry of dialogue and physical activity dominates the scene, the Archpriest briefly halts the action to confide to his reader that he is not totally unsympathetic to Fortune's predicament: "Oh, look at the poor wretch! Who that might have seen her just a few moments ago would have thought she'd be lying here conquered, half dead? I can't imagine anyone so cruel that he wouldn't shed a tear for her!" (GM, 266). Through dialogue, description, and personal intervention, then, Martínez creates two literary characters endowed with independent and opposing wills, two irreconcilable perspectives on reality in psychological and even physical conflict. However, this diversity in point of view is complicated all the more by his subjective commentary on the action. In this way, Boccaccio's narrative is dislodged from the one-dimensional world of allegory and made seemingly to co-exist with our author's own multifaceted reality; for the Archpriest contemplates his literary world from within, commenting upon it as if he were a material witness to the human struggle of Poverty and Fortune.

Action, dialogue, point of view, indeed characterization, are not the only embellishments contributed by Martínez to his source. He also amplifies ideas, varies and adds themes not found in Boccaccio's work. As we know, Part IV of the *Whip* is an essay affirming the doctrine of freedom of choice. As Boccaccio does in the *Fates of Illustrious Men*, Martínez uses the battle of Poverty and Fortune to exemplify this difficult concept. However, in the course of his narrative, the disputants become spokesmen for other important, albeit subordinate, moral and metaphysical beliefs. Thus in the *Archpriest of Talavera* Poverty is accorded a lengthy critical digression reminiscent of the *Danza general de la muerte* (*Universal Dance of Death*) and López de Ayala's *Rimado de Palacio* (*Palace Rhymes*). In this she bitterly chastises the churchmen who "desire the Pope's death so that their own candidate might succeed him," the "son who wishes death upon his father in order that he might be king and sovereign. The brother of the king who prays for his brother's demise so as to succeed to the throne, and the dukes, counts, courtiers, gentlemen, citizens, burghers, merchants, and artisans" wishing "death one upon the other, relatives as well as strangers, in order to inherit, acquire, and achieve a more important status" (GM, 255–56). The purpose of all this is a thorough condemnation of avarice ending in the assertion that "serving, loving, and pleasing God" (GM, 259) is the only worthwhile activity in life; this is Martínez's central theme, and one that is not openly expressed in the *Fates of Illustrious Men.*

The Archpriest cuts and adds to his sources, carefully fitting them into an organic narrative plan that makes continuous contrapuntal reference to his main theme—the love of God above everything. This concept serves as the unifying element of his work, the synthesizing agent of the disparate sources he employs. Through this common denominator Boccaccio and, as remains to be shown, Andreas Capellanus and a host of other sources are incorporated to form an orderly, well-structured, artistically original condemnation of worldly love.

II *Andreas and Martínez: from Essay to Fiction*

Anna Krause, while attempting to define the genre of the *Archpriest of Talavera,* associates Martínez's work with Andreas Capellanus's *De Amore Libri Tres* (*Art of Courtly Love*). Although she does not pursue the issue beyond saying that the latter "adduces arguments similar to those presented by the Archpriest to combat incontinence, and launches upon similar invective against woman and the sins commonly attributed to her by Churchmen in the Middle Ages—avarice, envy, slander, disobedience, pride, vanity, and so forth,"[11] she almost unwittingly hits upon the principal source of the *Whip.* Erich von Richthofen amplifies Miss Krause's marginal observations, proving not only that Martínez's work is very much like Andreas's famous book, but that the latter is indeed our author's most important and immediate model. He concludes that "Alfonso Martínez follows Book III of the *Art of Courtly Love,* the 'Rejection of Love,' as a source for the first and second parts of his work, copying entire passages of it, with some slight changes, almost word for word."[12] Book III of the *Art of Courtly Love* is in fact the frame upon which the first two parts of the *Whip* are built. However, as he did with Boccaccio, Martínez frequently adapts what he borrows from Andreas to suit his own purposes. While the "Rejection of Love" is a conclusion to Capellanus's work, it is the starting point and inspiration that is examined, glossed, varied, developed, and amplified in the Castilian masterpiece.

Capellanus plays a fundamental role in the creation of Martínez's work, for the *Art of Courtly Love* and the *Whip* both utilize as one of their most effective literary devices a one-sided "dialogue." Andreas addresses his troubled young friend, Walter, while our author converses with another disciple, his reader. Capellanus, for example, patiently directs his conversation to the young man in the following manner: "Now, friend Walter, if you will lend attentive ears to those things which after careful consideration we wrote down for you because you urged us so strongly, you can lack nothing in the art of love, since in this little book we gave you a theory of the subject, fully and completely, being willing to accede to your requests because of the great love we have for you."[13] This familiar tone is taken up by Martínez in Chapter 1 and is the recurring motif throughout Parts I and II of the *Archpriest of Talavera.* Martínez speaks to his reader in the second person familiar, establishing a constant dialogue well suited to his didactic designs: "Think, therefore, my brother, and with your fine understanding consider, what honor should be accorded him who, scorning his Lord and heavenly King, and scorning His commandment, gives himself to the devil, that enemy of God and His law, for a blind and wretched woman, or for his desire for her! You may well reflect, my friend, that if Our Lord God had desired that this sin of fornication might be committed without sin, He would not have ordained the celebration of marriage" (20). As von Richthofen points out, the moralizing tone of the Archpriest's work proves more severe than that in the "Rejection of Love."[14]

Martínez ably and liberally adapts themes, situations, and the dialogic structure from Andreas's book while at times reversing the order of the episodes and expanding the Latin passages to nearly three times their original length. Indeed, he so considerably modifies his source through amplification and digression that Capellanus's presence is barely noticeable. It is significant to note that modern criticism did not recognize the contribution of the "Rejection of Love" to the Castilian work until Anna Krause's essay in 1929. Had Martínez simply translated from the *Art of Courtly Love,* it is inconceivable that Menéndez y Pelayo, Arturo Farinelli, and other scholars would have failed to identify Andreas's influence. Our author was too accomplished an artist in his own right to be satisfied with a complete and literal transposition of the Latin work into Castilian. The dialogic structure and some of the motifs in Capellanus's third book become merely a framework upon which he builds a new and original tract of a totally different intention.

The Archpriest's chief artistic contribution to fifteenth-century Castilian literature lies in his use of dramatized exempla filled with rapid, direct, realistic dialogues and monologues. He amplifies almost every abstract concept adduced by Capellanus with a delightful, frequently ironic, dramatic scene. Von Richthofen perceives this essential difference and observes that the tales, with their use of colloquial language, are perhaps the work's principal literary merit.[15] A close examination of these anecdotes reveals much about Martínez and the nature of his eclectic art.

The most famous passages of the *Archpriest of Talavera* are probably the monologues of the women who lost the hen and the egg, appearing in almost every anthology of Spanish literature. These exempla are found in Part II, Chapter 1, a place in the narrative where Martínez, as Mario Penna notes, "follows the argument of the 'Rejection of Love,' but develops it with extraordinary originality and amplitude."[16] Altering the lineal development of Andreas's work, our author inverts the order in which these episodes are alluded to in the *Art of Courtly Love* and creates one of the most forceful and amusing scenes in early Spanish literature. Taking the following two declarative sentences from Andreas's work, Martínez invents two highly detailed, dramatic portraits that prefigure the verbal realism found a half century later in the *Celestina*:[17]

You can't find any woman so simple and foolish that she is unable to look out for her own property with a greedy tenacity, and with great mental subtlety get hold of the possessions of someone else. Indeed, even a simple woman is more careful about selling a single hen than the wisest lawyer is in dealing with a great castle (*Courtly Love,* 202)

Every woman is also loud-mouthed, since no one of them can keep her tongue from abuse, and if she loses a single egg she will keep up a clamor all day like a barking dog, and she will disturb the whole neighborhood over a trifle. (*Ibid.*, 207)

Stylistically, the highly original monologues of the two ranting women in the *Whip* are the direct predecessors of the narrative-dramatic technique María Rosa Lida de Malkiel describes under the chapter heading *La acotación* ("Dramatic Direction") in her *Originalidad artística de "La Celestina."*[18] Curiously, however, Mrs. Malkiel gives no credit to Martínez de Toledo for being the precursor of the method found in Fernando de Rojas's work.

Although our author's passage on the woman who had her egg stolen is a monologue, at first reading it gives the impression of a dialogue. The extraordinary abundance of interrogatives (more than half the sentences in the sequence) suggests the presence of another person whom the ranting woman is accusing. There are also numerous condemnatory exclamations evoking, along with the accumulation of questions, another character in the scene. Again and again the frantic woman exclaims:

What became of my egg? Who took it? Where is my egg? Although it was white, it is black and unlucky today! Whore and daughter of a whore, tell me who took my egg? Let whoever eats it be eaten by rabies! Alas, my egg of the double yolk, I was saving thee for hatching! Alas, my egg! What a cock and what a hen would have issued from thee! Of the cock I'd have made a capon worth twenty farthings, and the hen would have brought fourteen! Or perhaps I should have set her and she would have hatched out so many cockerels and pullets, and they would have so multiplied, that they would have got my feet out of the mud! But now I am luckless and poor as I was. Alas my lovely egg of the round tread and shell so thick! Who has eaten thee? Marica, you whore, you glutton, you have driven me out of my house! I swear I'll blister your cheeks for you, you low filthy pig! Alas, my egg! What will become of me now, poor forlorn wretch that I am! Jesus, my friend, why don't I die and get it over with? (103–104)

The expletives hurled at someone not yet identified ("Whore and daughter of a whore, tell me who took my egg?"), the later vocative use of a name "Marica, you whore . . .), plus the ironic description of the invoked person ("you glutton, you filthy pig") lead the reader to presume the physical presence of a character other than the screaming old crone. The second character remains silent throughout the tirade, but all the same we are led to feel her presence. It is inconsequential that no person is engaged in open dialogue with the frenetic old woman, for the very manner in which the scene is written supposes the existence, if not the active participation, of a silent interlocutor. Moreover, in this monologue the narrator's identity is completely overpowered by the forcefulness of his own creation. Martínez succumbs to art; abandoning all restraint, he loses control over the creatures of his imagination. Dialogue here is not only a tool of characterization but character itself. The erupting presence of the woman's self represents a first giant step toward the modern literary conception of personality—the invention of an autonomous and emphatic *I* that willfully confronts and eclipses a narrator's *me*.

Although Mrs. Malkiel explains similar monologues and dialogues in the *Celestina* in terms of the *comedia humanística* ("humanistic comedy"), another very possible source for the technique may indeed have been the *Archpriest of Talavera*. It is, we believe, unnecessary to look to Italian humanistic comedy for Rojas's precursors when the Spanish tradition itself offered him a literary master to emulate.

With the above in mind, we see how the Archpriest not only infuses Andreas's comparatively terse narrative with vivid, expansive, humanizing dialogue and monologue, but at once creates a new dramatic technique producing strong echoes in a later, extremely important, literary work. The passive, abstract statements of the *Art of Courtly Love* are vitalized and given immediacy, and are acted out by characters in open, impulsive conflict. Moreover, the characters in Martínez's exempla are not totally flat. Their intense, colloquial, exclamatory, and interrogative harangues transcend the written word to suggest people, things, and situations beyond the work itself. Martínez dramatically evokes, rather than narrates, a world populated with living beings whose high-spirited presence is felt but not overtly described. It is here that the celebrated realism of the *Whip* is rooted: instead of recounting a dialogue ("he said this, the other said that"), Martínez allows his characters to directly confront each other and speak for themselves. Their undirected voices prod the reader's imagination to intuit their emotional states and their surroundings. It is precisely this quality that leads Dámaso Alonso to describe the art of the *Archpriest of Talavera* as an "intuitive unfolding of the human soul through the means of direct speech."[19]

Martínez's main modification of his literary sources lies in stylistic change and shrewd observation, and in his allowing free rein to his fecund imagination. These qualities are complicated by his varying, reorganizing, glossing, and digressing upon the concepts of Capellanus's "Rejection of Love." In the first place, there is a fundamental difference in attitude between the two works; for our author's vision of worldly love is essentially ascetic, placing his emphasis almost entirely on the adverse doctrinal consequences of carnality. Carnal passion is sin, sin goes against the will of God and therefore leads to eternal damnation. Expressing the same idea as Saint Paul (1 Corinthians, 7:2–7), and following a strictly orthodox Christian view, Martínez tells us "that so grave is this sin of carnality that even those who are united in God's ordained matrimony indulge themselves so excessively that they can hardly avoid committing sin" (36).

While Andreas makes a similar statement in his "Rejection of Love" (*Courtly Love*, 188), he nevertheless advocates a disciplined eroticism, *amor mixtus* ("mixed love," or a synthesis of the sensual and spiritual forms of love), accepting it as a fact of life and even a form of virtue. In Books I and II, he goes so far as to intimate that physical possession is the ultimate end of all relationships, and that true love is always essentially adulterous. For Capellanus, courtship becomes almost a sport and one of the few earthly goods bestowed upon man, albeit he notes in passing that *amor purus* ("pure love," or devotion between a man and a woman free of sexual concerns) is the highest form of love. Moreover, as von Richthofen points out, in Book III he concedes a soothing effect to love, provided one goes about it properly.[20] Andreas does, however, allude to unrestrained passion as a form of bestiality leading to man's perdition, although when condemning it he opts for underlining its secular consequences—virtually limiting himself to abstractly describing its spiritual evils: "If you abstain from it, the Heavenly King will be more favorably disposed toward you in every respect, and you will be worthy to have all prosperous success in this world and to fulfill all praiseworthy deeds and the honorable desires of your heart, and in the world to come have glory and life everlasting" (*Courtly Love*, 211).

The Archpriest, in contrast, spends all of Part I of the *Whip* carefully dramatizing how worldly love, be it tempered or not, is the prime mover of chaos and how it transgresses every moral and religious doctrine: how it violates the Ten Commandments (61–77); is the cause for committing the seven deadly sins (77–87); and is contrary to the four cardinal virtues (87–97). It is not until he has proven this through illustrative anecdotes that he resoundingly concludes that "all evils proceed from love" (97), reaffirming his central thesis that "we must love only Him and leave behind us and forget the transitory things of this world, because by truly loving Him, and loving His infinite glory, there is no doubt that we shall attain it forever and ever" (12). Totally rejecting the temporal benefits afforded by abstention as outlined by Andreas (prosperity, honor, and the fulfillment of the heart's desires), Martínez looks only to the Kingdom of God. He calls for complete adoration of the Creator, even eschewing Capellanus's definition of "pure love," or a man's spiritual worship of a woman. Indeed, as we shall see later, our author considers purely spiritual human relationships a form of idolatry. Put simply, the *Art of Courtly Love* accepts a restrained form of *eros* ("physical love") but prefers *philos* (a "spiritual" but nevertheless human love), while the *Archpriest of Talavera* repudiates both of these and counsels only *agapé* ("divine love").

In the course of demonstrating the metaphysical evils of all forms of human passion, Martínez is often sidetracked, continually digressing upon subordinate themes sometimes unconsciously suggested to him by his Latin source. For Andreas, a simple abstract imprecation against woman's vanity and love's sinful ways is sufficient. The Archpriest, however, is not content with a trite censure of feminine vainglory and concupiscence.

Rather, he prefers to drive home the point by dramatizing these themes, novelistically analyzing their motives and consequences, indeed their every facet.

Satisfied only in declaring the innate pretentiousness of women, for example, Capellanus succinctly states that "you cannot find a woman so lowly-born that she will not tell you she has famous relatives and is descended from a family of great men and who will not make all sorts of boasts about herself" (*Courtly Love*, 206–207). Martínez uses this statement to launch an original digression, not only on feminine social climbing and vanity, but on the deception of appearances in general. He accordingly transcends the thematic boundaries imposed upon him by the "Rejection of Love," narrating a humorous, graphic, almost picaresque episode in which a woman borrows gowns, livery, and even cosmetics so as to parade through the streets putting on airs. Constantly calling attention to herself during her brief whirl in the sphere of appearances, she belittles her borrowed raiment and exclaims at every step of the way: "Lord, what a bad saddle! Lord, what a mule! I'm shaken to a jelly! It trots and doesn't know how to walk! My hand hurts from holding it back, poor wretch that I am! I'm beaten to a pulp! What will become of me?" (144). In this scene worthy of Quevedo's don Pablos, in addition to plumbing the depths of mock self-pity, Martínez explores the favorite Hispanic theme of perspectivism, severely concluding that being (*ser*) and seeming (*parecer*) are indeed two very different things.

The few textual comparisons we have made between the *Archpriest of Talavera* and its two most immediate sources, the *Fates of Illustrious Men* and the *Art of Courtly Love,* reveal that its author was an extraordinary raconteur of original and creative talent whose capacity for literary invention led him to portray new situations from the hackneyed hand-baggage of medieval didactic texts. Stylistically, Martínez proves his forceful artistic independence from the Latin models, rendering his work in a rich, natural language that vividly defines the characters populating his fictive world. In short, he creatively adapts these sources to his own unique ends, selecting appropriate passages of Latin prose and converting them into equally instructive scenes of more effective dramatic action, thematic complexity, and didactic efficacy. When filtered through the imagination and pen of Alfonso Martínez de Toledo, the clichés of medieval literature acquire a youthfulness and vigor not attained in their original form.

III *The* Secrets of Old Philosophers

Naturally there were other influences affecting Martínez when he wrote the *Whip*. Part III of his work, where he attempts to establish the relationship between the physical and moral characteristics of men according to their birth signs, is almost entirely based on the pseudo-science of physiognomy. Almost as old as recorded history, physiognomy, or the relationship of physique and personality, developed as a branch of natural science and medicine, and today is still considered valid by some psychologists. Like most ancient knowledge, the earliest treatment of the subject was attributed to Aristotle.[21] During the Middle Ages the study of the interdependency of character and physical features merged with astrology and was accepted as a legitimate form of medical psychology and moral philosophy.[22]

The astrobiological theories of love which the Archpriest expounds in Part III of the *Whip* are grounded in a popular medieval treatise partially dealing with physiognomy and cosmology—the pseudo-Aristotelian *Secreta Secretorum* (*Secrets of Old Philosophers*). This work is supposedly a book of wisdom written by Aristotle for Alexander the Great, and represents a primary source for the medieval admonitory essays on the governance of princes. Although the *Secrets of Old Philosophers* is, of course, by no means the only medieval authority dealing with medical astrology,[23] we may surmise it was the one used by Martínez to form the theoretical basis of Part III of the *Archpriest of Talavera*. Speaking of the body's indications of personality, he tells us that "you will find the matter treated at length in the book called *De secretis secretorum*, which Aristotle wrote for Alexander, near the end of it" (175).

The influence of the *Secrets* on the *Whip* is, however, far more diffuse than that of the previously mentioned sources. Martínez does not seem to have had the text at hand, recalling, condensing, and incorporating only broad ideas, while ignoring specific textual allusions or translations. Indeed, explaining how birth signs affect not only the general temperament of individuals but even certain parts of their bodies, he gives the impression of not being wholly conversant with the subject. Without further explanation, at one point he simply enumerates the signs of the zodiac and the corresponding body parts they influence. In his catalogue, he blatantly omits Aquarius, a masculine sign exercising dominion over the lower legs, and gives the impression of treading unfamiliar, or at least distantly recalled, ground (174). Apparently unsure of his subject, moreover, he quickly excuses himself from pursuing it further for fear "lest they who read this should quarrel with one another" (175).

The chapters on physiognomy in the *Secrets* explain the relation of a great many physical features to an equally vast number of personality traits. An upright stature, for example, is interpreted as a sign of measured reason; a deep voice, an indication of gravity; broad shoulders, courage; thin thighs, ignorance; small eyes, cowardice; and so on. Through a composite of these, the work attempts to categorize man's physique into temperaments and thereby predict his talents for dealing with a number of given situations—most notably his ability to govern. On the other hand, in consonance with his disparagement of worldly love, Martínez recalls and exaggerates only the erotic and sexual inferences of the four temperaments described in the earlier work. Moreover, displaying his fondness for literary invention, he dramatically adapts and exemplifies the amatory inclinations of the types outlined in it. Phlegmatic, sanguine, melancholy, and choleric men are each accorded elaborate exempla picturing their conduct in love situations. Martínez turns the cosmological abstractions of the *Secrets* into humorous scenes overflowing with the kind of characters, dialogues, irony, and psychological depth we have already had occasion to discuss.

There is one point, however, on which he closely follows the reasoning of the *Secrets*. Like it, he argues that celestial physiognomy can only point out man's predisposition for certain forms of behavior, never fatalistically predict it. The dominion of the stars applies only to the body, for the soul is always free to counteract the heavens' influence. The soul possesses the power to distinguish between good and evil: the wise man recognizes the inherent inclinations of his nature, choosing a course that leads him from sin. The Archpriest's arguments illustrating the applicability of this to worldly love might well have been inspired by the story of Philemon the physiognomist, found in all medieval versions of the *Secrets*. In this exemplum, Hippocrates' disciples take a portrait of their master to Philemon so that he may interpret it according to his science. Philemon tells the students that the likeness is that of someone by nature lecherous and deceptive. Irate, the students threaten to kill him for his slander of the physician. Philemon quickly replies that his diagnosis represents only the natural disposition of the man in the portrait, and not necessarily his true manner. Later, the disciples relate the incident to Hippocrates himself, who concurs with Philemon's findings. Affirming the soul's preeminence over matter, he notes that while he is indeed inherently inclined to lechery, his free will triumphs over his natural disposition.[24] To say, however, that Part III of the *Whip* is inspired solely by this anecdote dealing with carnality would be an oversimplification. Many other concepts of physiognomy and astrology dispersed in the *Secrets* are analogous to Martínez's, although he consistently limits their application only to the conduct of men in love.

The Archpriest, then, selects information from the *Secrets* in order to prove his thesis that only weak men are inclined by the stars toward lust. There is, he grants, a natural influence of the heavenly bodies over man's physical makeup. but it cannot be considered deterministic. Preparing us for the last part of the *Whip,* in which he explicitly argues the primacy of the will over matter, in Part III he uses the astrobiological theories of the *Secrets of Old Philosophers* to implicitly reaffirm his belief that worldly love is indeed a willful and punishable sin.

IV *Saint Augustine: Nature, God, Love, and Will*

Part IV of the *Archpriest of Talavera* is an orthodox scholastic essay affirming the Christian doctrine of free will. Like most medieval works dealing with this subject, it is based on the teachings of the Church Fathers, most notably Saint Augustine.

Martínez derives his argument against predestination, and indeed a great many of his metaphysical beliefs, almost wholly from Augustine. Erich von Richthofen feels he may also have been influenced by Saint Thomas Aquinas and Saint Pedro Pascual, although our author never mentions either of them in his work.[25] An examination of Aquinas's and Pascual's teachings reveals that their common ground with Martínez is simply a censure of fatalism, a traditional posture originating with Augustine and shared by all orthodox Christian theologians.[26]

Martínez's metaphysics has a distinct Augustinian bent, and is most firmly grounded in the saint's *De Doctrina Christiana* (*On Christian Doctrine*) and *De Libero Arbitrio* (*On Free Choice of the Will*). The former was the most widely disseminated and often used patristic authority against fatalism in the Middle Ages, and was probably Martínez's principal source in his wholesale reproach of judicial astrology. Like Augustine (*Christian Doctrine*, Book II, Chapters 21, 22), our author is emphatic in his indictment of the belief that the stars determine and can foretell the course of men's lives. It is, he says, a "bad and pernicious opinion which many people hold as truth, although reproved by the Holy Mother Church" (GM, 207). Despite this outright repudiation, however, he notes, almost in the same breath, that he "does not deny that superior bodies influence inferior ones, and that people born on certain days and hours receive qualities and correspondences inclined by the planets" (GM, 208).

If this may seem paradoxical, it is not so when viewed in terms of the Augustinian conception of the universe. While in the first declaration Martínez condemns the deterministic interpretation of the heavens as emphatically as the saint, in the second he admits to the existence of a universal order and a hierarchy of higher and lower realities in nature. Like Augustine, he maintains that as a part of nature man is, of course, subject to this natural order and cannot escape it. However, he is endowed with a soul (comprised of reason, intellect, and will) enabling him to controvert it. Man's physical being may be subject to the predisposition of the stars, a higher form of natural reality, but his spirit cannot be forced to conform with their compulsions. Moreover, both profess that this natural order exists only because God, the supreme Creator, has willfully imposed it (see *Free Choice of the Will*, Book III, Chapter 11, and *Epistles*, 140, 2 and 4). "Our Lord," Martínez says, "is the one and only mover of all things. From this it follows that fates, planets, signs, and fortune lack this power, and that they are in fact governed by Him, orbiting and performing their functions only with His permission" (GM, 255). Almighty God, if He wills it so, then, may even nullify the stars' dominion over man. And indeed, the self-sufficient Deity has done just that, providing man, through His infinite love, with freedom of choice (synonymous with the will in Augustinian terms). However, in choosing, man must distinguish between good and evil (see *Free Choice of the Will*, Book II, Chapters 2, 18): "Each person is his own master and has within him the God-given grace to do good or evil" (GM, 212). In exercising this divine gift man proves himself deserving of eternal damnation or salvation. Therefore, the excuse that one lusts because he is fated to do so is naive and a sin of volition (see *Free Choice of the Will*, Book I, Chapters 10, 11).

An omnipotent, loving God is also always present and all knowing: "Wherever we go, whatever we say, we are never out of God's reach" (GM, 231), Martínez tells us, echoing Saint Augustine (*Christian Doctrine*, Book I, Chapter 12). If this raises the problem of His prescience, hence implying a form of predestination, his arguments are similar to Augustine's (*Free Choice of the Will*, Book III, Chapters 2, 3) in that God, since he has bestowed his grace on man, "will never contradict or retract the creature's ability to choose freely" (GM, 214). As Saint Augustine observes, "the power [to will] is not taken from me by His foreknowledge; but because of His foreknowledge, the power to will will more certainly be present in me, since God, whose foreknowledge does not err, has foreknown that I shall have the power" (*Free Choice of the Will*, Book III, Chapter 3). Moreover, God in His infinite knowledge and truth possesses secrets (*Christian Doctrine*, Book II, Chapter 23) beyond man's comprehension (GM, 243). Taking a distinctly anti-Thomistic stance, Martínez says he "cannot define the actions of God; they are not subject to sophisms, obligatories, *terminus ad quem*, Llullist arguments, or syllogisms, only to His Will;

what He wants and permits" (GM, 210). In the strictest Augustinian terms, God must be approached only through faith. Realizing that His plans are always for the good, one must accept His ways on faith alone. Furthermore, Scripture plays a paramount role in revealing His accessible judgments (see *Christian Doctrine*, Book IV, Chapter 8). On these points Martínez seems to go beyond Augustine, and he expounds a theology coming curiously close to Duns Scotus's *voluntarism* and William of Occam's *skepticism*.

Scotism virtually destroyed the Thomistic compromise of reason and revelation, for Duns logically determined that will moves the intellect, since it has no other cause than itself; not vice versa, as Aquinas asserted.[27] Occam developed this clever distinction of the Scotsman's philosophy to a point where he held that reason and revelation must, by definition, be separate and impenetrable spheres. He insisted that faith could no longer be held to supplement reason, since it was rationally possible to prove the contradictory nature of certain dogmas—one of which was free will (see *Quodlibeta Septem*, I, q. 16). Although faith is thus shown to be irrational, it must nevertheless be followed because it is supreme and reason irrelevant in a theological interpretation of the universe. In short, Occam maintains a skepticism about natural knowledge and man's reason, since God the Creator and Mover is Himself unknowable through human inquiry. This philosophic posture at once dismissed the great medieval scholastic *Summas*, which so heavily depended on the primacy of the intellect.[28]

In the last part of the *Archpriest of Talavera* the conflict of reason and revelation is implicit. Although Martínez actively opposes determinism, he nevertheless seems to contradict himself when he states that "Almighty God, if he wishes, can decree against you and me and counter against my disposition as well as yours; although we might want to act wickedly, it pleases Him that we be good" (GM, 208–209). He clearly inverts his own rational conclusions on free will. This, however, is no lapse on our author's part, for in the course of his analytical disputation in favor of freedom of choice, he affirms, as we have said, the unknowable and secret nature of God. Martínez, in the end, emphasizes the futility of rationally explaining freedom of choice:

not just once, but three times, he underscores the impossibility of attempting to define God and His ways, repeating that the mysteries of the Creator are unfathomable and should be accepted on faith alone. Berating those who question God's judgments, for example, he emphasizes reason's inefficacy and exclaims: "Leave, leave God's secrets alone; you should not desire to scrutinize them or know what or why they are" (GM, 220). For Martínez de Toledo, theological knowledge is a matter of faith and will, not logic.

The Christian theological process from Augustine to Thomas Aquinas symbolized the gradual conciliation of reason and faith; the triumph of the intellect that expressed the unity of man with his Creator. For the great medieval doctors of the Church, God was rational, familiar, accessible, and knowable. For William of Occam, and it would seem Martínez de Toledo, He was willful, withdrawn, and enigmatic, the unmoved Mover "people should not think or dispute about" (GM, 212).

Nevertheless, the theologian with the most preponderant influence on Martínez remains Saint Augustine, and his most telling derivation from the saint's teachings is his view of love. Throughout the *Whip* Martínez never once proposes that man should stop loving. On the contrary, he sees love as part of man's essence. The question for him, as for Augustine, is not whether man should love, but what he should love. And for both, man's will determines the value of his love. Hence, if his will is good, his passions and his love are equally good; if his will is evil, they will also be evil: *recta itaque voluntas est bonus amor et voluntas perversa malus amor* ("therefore a virtuous will is good love, a perverse will bad love").[29] Augustine coincides with Martínez's distinction of divine love and "disordered love" (*amor desordenado*), consistently calling for what he terms "rightly ordered love" (see *City of God*, XV, 22). In his *On Christian Doctrine*, the saint identifies this as the love of God (Book I, Chapters 22–29), and lust as the source of all evil in *On Free Choice of the Will* (Book I, Chapter 3). For both authors, the will is a God-given grace that should naturally be exercised in loving Him, although He does not force man's volition to do so. Good love is the will to love God, bad love, the will to lust.

Martínez's views on nature, God, love, and freedom of the will are orthodox and traditional, reflecting an intimate familiarity with Augustine's teachings on the subjects. In addition, in his discussion of freedom of choice and its relation to love, he includes concepts from the *Compendium Theologicae Veritatis* (*Compendium of Theological Truth*), exempla inspired in the *Corpus Juris Canonicis* (*Body of Canon Law*), and quotations from the *Psalms* and the *Breviarium Romanum* (*Roman Breviary*).[30] But, in sum, the underlying direction of his metaphysical views is derived almost wholly from Saint Augustine, whom he names on seven different occasions.

V *Secondary Sources: Authorities and Wisdom Literature*

Throughout the Middle Ages it was common practice for a writer to quote or allude to *auctores* or *auctoritates* (authors or works that were universally acknowledged authorities on a subject). A phenomenon originating in the philosophical and canon law tracts of the Schoolmen, it was carried over into lay literature and employed by writers until the end of the medieval period to lend credence to their arguments. Alfonso Martínez was no exception. Utilizing this familiar artifice in the *Whip*, at certain points he cites such diverse authors as Socrates (Part III, Chapter 8), Ovid (Part III, Chapter 9), Ostiense (Henry of Susa) (Part III, Chapter 9), Peter Lombard (Part I, Chapter 30), pseudo-Cato (Part II, Chapter 4; Part III, Chapter 8; and three times in Part IV, Chapters 1, 2, 3), Valerius Maximus (Part IV, Chapter 2), Petrarch (Part II, Chapters 4, 9), Saint Isidore of Seville (Part III, Chapter 9), and Françesc Eiximenis (Part IV, Chapter 1).

A comparison with Book III of the *Art of Courtly Love* reveals that Martínez also often refers to authorities cited in this work, making it seem as if he had firsthand knowledge of the authors Andreas cites. This is the case with Johannitius (whose *Isagoge Iohannicii ad Artem Parvum Galeni* he mentions in Part I, Chapter 16 of the *Whip*), Cicero (Part I, Chapter 3), Martianus Capella (Part II, Chapter 5), and Ptolemy (Part II, Chapters 7, 8).[31]

Revealing his familiarity with Scripture and canon law literature, on several occasions he gives authority to his disputation on freedom of choice by referring the reader to the Bible and works like the *Clementine Constitutions* (see Part III, Chapters 7, 8), *Gratian's Decree* (see Part IV, Chapters 1, 3), the *Extra Decrees* of Gregory IX (Part I, Chapter 15; Part IV, Chapter 1), and Gregory the Great's *Morals on the Book of Job* (Part I, Chapter 30; Part IV, Chapter 1). Although he again attempts to give the impression of a direct knowledge of these authorities, most can be found dispersed throughout the *Compendium of Theological Truth* and the *Body of Canon Law,* two books Martínez was definitely familiar with and probably had at hand when writing the *Archpriest of Talavera.*[32]

None of the authors or works we have cited here can truly be considered primary sources for the *Whip.* Rather, they reflect medieval literature's practice of artful name-dropping: the sentiment that if one cites a respected source, accurately or inaccurately (Martínez's references are often incorrect), it will lend extra weight and credibility to the conclusions the author reaches. The manner in which Martínez supports his theses with authorities recalls the corroborative technique taught students of canon and civil law during the Middle Ages. In fact, evidence of the Archpriest's knowledge of legal terminology and rhetoric appears throughout his work (see, for example, Part I, Chapter 37).

Martínez's views on worldly and divine love were sufficiently codified that he probably would have expressed them in the same manner, regardless of the texts he alludes to in buttressing his argument. Nevertheless, his use of authorities is significant because it reveals that he was a well-read cleric able to summon philosophical and theological precedents from diverse writings in his attempt to convince his readers of the sinful nature of lust. He adopts the use of authorities in his work in an effort to strive for soundness. In his day, the corroborative method of the Scholastics seemed, after all, the best and most convincing form of argumentation.

VI *The Two Archpriests*

As we know, Martínez was a well-traveled, university-educated cleric, and from the kinds of sources already discussed we may assume he was thoroughly familiar with the theological, didactic, and humanistic currents of his age. He was, of course, also well schooled in the Castilian literary tradition. A chief influence on the *Whip* was Juan Ruiz's *Libro de buen amor* (*Book of Good Love*). Indeed, artistically, structurally, and thematically the *Archpriest of Talavera* closely follows the earlier work. These two authors have frequently been compared. In the eighteenth century, for instance, Tomás Antonio Sánchez declared that "the Archpriest of Talavera is as good a writer of prose as the Archpriest of Hita is of verse."[33] Menéndez y Pelayo notes that both succeed in capturing "everything the eye beholds."[34] In each we find the popular preacher's instinct for the graphic. One need only compare the sense of fun, plasticity, movement, force, and artistic revelry of Hita's battle of don Carnal and doña Cuaresma to Martínez's struggle of Poverty and Fortune to recognize their kinship.

Apart from similar exploitation of graphic images, however, our author's work betrays evidence of a direct textual dependence on the *Book of Good Love*. On several occasions Martínez's context is analogous to Ruiz's, and he quotes proverbs from him. He tells us, for example, that "'he who can be his own master, let him not sell himself, for liberty and freedom are not bought for gold.' This is an ancient saying the Archpriest of Hita put into his treatise" (26). Martínez's reference is to stanza 206 of the *Book of Good Love*: "He who is not oppressed should not seek tyranny: / Liberty and freedom cannot be bought for gold" (*El que non toviere premia, non quiera ser apremiado: / Lybertad é soltura non es por oro conplado*).[35] In Part III, Chapter 8, after citing other authorities, notably pseudo-Cato and Ovid, Martínez tells us that "the Archpriest of Hita says: 'It is wisdom to keep a temperate silence and folly to talk too much'" (185). Although Martín de Riquer denies that the proverb is contained in the *Book of Good Love*,[36] our author could have been misquoting from memory and thinking of couplet 568. It expresses a similar sentiment: "Just as you keep food in your stomach, / Keep a secret, something more digestible: Cato, the Roman sage, demands it in his book, / He says that good friends keep secrets" (*Como tyn' tu estomago en sy mucha vyanda, / Tenga la poridat, que es mucho más blanda: / Catón, sabyo rromano, en su lybro lo manda, / Diz' que la poridat en buen amigo anda*). While not exactly identical to Martínez's citation, the fact that Ruiz's stanza counsels secrecy (a form of silence) and mentions pseudo-Cato might indicate that the later author was thinking of this couplet. Another passage in the *Whip* perhaps recalling the *Book of Good Love* is the statement that "another reason you should eschew love is that an infinity of deaths and unnumbered wars ensue from it, and many peaces are broken, as I have said, because of unbridled love of women. Thus we see cities, castles, villages destroyed by love, and we may see many rich men ruined because of it" (42). Alluding to Genesis 19–24, the Archpriest of Hita makes a similar declaration: "On account of lust five cities were / Burned and destroyed, three of them because of wickedness" (*Ffueron por la loxuria çinco nobles çibdades / Quemadas e destruydas, las tres por sus maldades*; stanza 260).

However, the relationship of both authors goes well beyond Martínez's citing Ruiz as an authority in typically medieval fashion, for in addition to the quotations and possible allusions to Ruiz we have pointed out above, Martínez occasionally makes direct reference to characters in the *Book of Good Love*. The woman in the famous lost egg monologue, for example, calls to her servant girl to enlist Trotaconventos to help her search for it (106). Trotaconventos is Juan Ruiz's go-between who arranges the amorous adventures in his work.

Moreover, the *Book of Good Love* and Part I of the *Archpriest of Talavera* share a common external structure. The two works attempt to exemplify the breaking of the Ten Commandments and the commission of the seven deadly sins in the pursuit of lust. While this, of course, may be attributed to both authors' sermonically glossing the catechism in developing their arguments, the similarity and order in which the exempla appear suggest Ruiz's influence on Martínez. In Part I, Chapter 17, for instance, our author's exemplum retelling the biblical story of David and Bathsheba (2 Samuel 11: 6–27) may have been inspired by the *Book of Good Love*, or by a common source, since in both it is immediately followed by a variant of the anecdote recounting Vergil's deception at the hands of the ladylove who left him hanging from a tower (*Good Love,* stanzas 258–67).

Apart from these textual similarities, the two works also share a theme of fundamental importance: the dialectic of worldly and divine love. The medieval mind was inclined to function in terms of irreconcilably opposed forces (God/Devil, Jew/Christian, Water/Wine, Elena/María). However, until this time in Castilian literature, only Ruiz and Martínez openly saw the world operating specifically in terms of carnality and divine love. In fact, the *Whip's* distinction between worldly love (*amor mundano*) and divine love (*amor de Dios*) appears to offer no more than variants of the thematic opposites of good love (*buen amor*) and mad love (*loco amor*) as distinguished in the *Book of Good Love* and articulated centuries earlier in the writings of Saint Augustine. Furthermore, both authors view carnal passion as a physically debilitating force, a power leading to the soul's damnation and the violation of every moral and religious law. Similarly, each seems to identify worldly love as a cult in direct conflict, indeed competition, with Christianity. Juan Ruiz, for example, tacitly accuses the allegorical character don Amor ("Master Love") of profaning Catholic ritual, notably the Canonical Hours (stanzas 374–89),[37] while Martínez demonstrates how lovers worshiping their ladies in place of God disobey His First Commandment, concluding that "the love of a man for a woman, or that of a woman for a man, is founded upon sin" (63). He also notes that "love is . . . the cause of our worshiping strange gods and idolatry" (34–35).

Because of its seemingly contradictory nature, Ruiz's work is unclear as to which form of love it counsels. Although, like Martínez's, it ostensibly advises only the love of God "because the world is vanity" (stanza 105), it is full of ambiguities, retractions, and turnabouts, and appears to be more the anguished expression of a man caught in the middle of the tension existing between carnality and spiritual love. Recent opinion suggests that Ruiz might have been parodying the conventions of courtly love, satirically adopting Andreas Capellanus's treatise in an effort to combat the Frenchman's theses.[38] If this was in fact his intention, it is possible that Martínez saw through the ambiguity (if it even existed for him) of the *Book of Good*

Love and decided to take up where Ruiz left off, glossing Andreas's "Rejection of Love" while looking to Hita as a moral authority who had trod similar ground a century before. The Archpriest of Hita, as we have seen, is twice mentioned directly in the *Whip*, and possibly alluded to on several other occasions. His book, like our author's, glosses the Decalogue and the seven deadly sins, repudiates judicial astrology (stanzas 123–60) with similar arguments, and attempts to clarify the fatalistic implications of physiognomy often adduced in the late Middle Ages to apologize for sinful love's inevitability.[39] Moreover, the *Book of Good Love* is significantly the only Castilian source thought worthy of mention in Martínez's exuberant and sincere reproach of worldly love. Indeed, we feel our author even titled his tract the *Archpriest of Talavera* in homage to Ruiz's work, which was commonly referred to as the *Book of the Archpriest of Hita* during the fourteenth and fifteenth centuries.[40]

While the *Book of Good Love* served as an important influence on the *Whip*, the latter work is equally important in attempting to decipher the meaning of Ruiz's treatise. Written barely a century later, the *Archpriest of Talavera* seems in many respects a liberal gloss of the *Book of Good Love*. Indeed, the textual, thematic, and temporal proximity of the two suggests that Martínez's work may be an unambiguous elaboration of Juan Ruiz's purpose. Future endeavors to decipher the meaning of the earlier tract should not overlook the fact that the *Whip* appears to afford a medieval perspective upon its message. Perhaps if the *Book of Good Love* is approached through the eyes of Alfonso Martínez, the question of its long-argued didacticism may be resolved.

VII *The Popular Tradition*

Up to this point we have limited our discussion to the cultivated, bookish sources of the Archpriest's treatise, confirming that "it is a testimonial to his vast reading."[41] We shall now turn to the popular tale in the *Whip*. Many of the edifying concepts Martínez borrowed from Boccaccio, Andreas, the Church Fathers, Juan Ruiz, medieval wisdom literature, and theological compendia are illustrated by exempla he chose from the popular tradition. Although the great majority of the tales in the work seem to be from personal experience,[42] Martínez was a typical medieval writer in that he also sought inspiration in folk legends and stories.

Von Richthofen has identified three categories of tales and anecdotes in the work: (1) legends and exempla with classical motifs (for example, Aristotle being humiliated by his mistress, Part I, Chapter 17); (2) those derived from the compilations used by the preachers (the blinded husband, and the hidden priest, Part II, Chapter 10); and (3) those invented by Martínez but inspired by his Latin sources (for instance, Irazón the painter, Part I, Chapter 24).[43] He points out analogues to the tales in such diverse works as Peter Alphonsus's *Clerical Instruction*, the *Gesta Romanorum* (*The Deeds of the Romans*), the *Art of Courtly Love*, the *Fates of Illustrious Men*, French *fabliaux*, the Spanish ballad tradition, and the *Body of Canon Law*. It must be added, however, that these tales were so abundant during the Middle Ages that to specify any one particular source, unless both versions are identical in every detail, is quite risky and probably inaccurate. As Kenneth Jackson warns, "when we are dealing with literatures in which oral telling is known or believed with good reason to have played a very large part we ought not to assume that some particular version known to us—call it B—of any given story is directly derived from version A unless there is some definite and irrefutable piece of evidence other than identity of plot to prove that version B does actually come from version A and not from some third version now lost."[44] Nevertheless, brief comparisons of a few of Martínez's exempla and some of their medieval variants are warranted in order to underline our author's familiarity with the folk tradition and his genius for literary invention and adaptation.

Martínez's anecdote depicting a husband's murder of his wife is clearly inspired in Capellanus's "Rejection of Love," although, as we shall see, it also bears a close resemblance to tale twenty-seven of Juan Manuel's *Conde Lucanor* (*Tales of Count Lucanor*). Andreas alludes to this popular motif in his effort to exemplify the disobedience of women:

We read, too, of a very wise man who had a wife whom he hated. Because he wanted to avoid killing her with his own hand, and he knew that some women always strive eagerly after what is forbidden them, he prepared a very valuable flask into which he put wine of the best and most fragrant kind, mixed with poison, and he said to his wife, "My sweetest wife, be careful not to touch this vessel, and don't venture to taste any of the liquor, because it is poisonous and deadly to human beings." But the woman scorned her husband's prohibition, for no sooner had he gone away than she drank some of the forbidden liquor and so died of the poison. (*Courtly Love*, 205)

A comparison between this version and Martínez's (133–36) reveals that the plot is the same, except that our author complicates it and creates intricate characters who speak and act out the action. Indeed, Martínez elaborates Andreas's synopsis of this popular tale until it becomes a short character study and a profound lesson in morality—not simply a vindictive example of murder motivated by woman's odious curiosity. The fundamental difference in Martínez's variant is the inclusion of the theme of lust, for the husband kills his wife on account of her infidelity. By now it is obvious that the Archpriest sees concupiscence as the root of every evil, and in adapting this tale to fit the main theme of his treatise he accordingly makes adultery the prime motive for the woman's death. In this way, he displays a concern for thematic harmony and a desire to rationalize his character's behavior.

Martínez must have been familiar with more elaborate versions of the story than Andreas's. In fact, he may even have known the variant we have mentioned in *Count Lucanor*. In Juan Manuel's tale, the Emperor Fadrique has an obstinate wife who never complies with his wishes. Indeed, whatever he wills, she does the opposite. One day, just as he is going off to hunt, the Emperor shows a poisonous herb to her, warning her in front of witnesses not to put it on any part of her body. Before leaving, Fadrique rubs a harmless ointment on some sores and tells his wife she can use this if she needs any medication. He then takes some of the poisonous herb for the arrows that are to be used in the hunt. Upon seeing this, the Empress is convinced that the so-called poison is an ointment of great healing powers her husband wants to conceal from her. To spite Fadrique, she rubs herself with the deadly mixture "and much to her sorrow died because of her stubborn manner."[45]

If Martínez did not know this version directly, he was certainly familiar with a close variant. Both he and Juan Manuel make a point to note that the husband warns his wife before witnesses who could act in his defense should he be accused of murder. Moreover, in the *Whip* and *Count Lucanor* the action is situated in a distant land, each author emphasizes the beauty and noble lineage of the woman, and the murdering husband is described as a wise ruler. The only noticeable difference between the two versions is the use of an ointment in the earlier text instead of wine, and Martínez's insistence upon establishing a motive for the crime.

Contrasting the three variants of this motif we find that the *Art of Courtly Love* version is in reality a plot summary. The *Count Lucanor* exemplum is similar to the *Whip*'s in that it specifies locale, witnesses, and the social position of culprit and victim; but it does not approach the degree of literary sophistication we find in our author's rendition. The simple unanalyzed act of hatred in the earlier versions becomes a psychologically well-motivated crime of passion in Martínez's work. Resorting to direct speech, Martínez enters the mind of the villainous husband and creates a literary portrait in which he unmasks his character's calculating personality. Carefully weighing the pros and cons of executing his unfaithful wife, the cuckolded husband reasons in the following manner:

> If I kill her I will ruin myself, for she has two things on her side: justice and her kinsmen, who will proceed against me; justice, because no man should take the law into his own hands without knowledge of it and without proper witnesses, worthy of credence, and good depositions, with notarized instruments and documents—all this in the presence of the president, governor, magistrate, or regent of the king's court. Moreover, one ought not avenge himself or punish anyone at all by his own hand. I cannot, therefore, proceed without depositions, for her kinsmen would say, besides, that I brought these charges in order to kill her and take another wife, and they would be my enemies. (133)

After lengthy consideration of the stain on his honor and the possible legal consequences of publicly accusing his wife, he decides not to kill her by his own hand or by recourse to the law. He thus conjures up the scheme of the poisoned wine. When the deed is done, furthermore, Martínez delves more deeply into the murderer's character, for he tells us of both his private and his public reactions to his wife's death: "When the husband heard the shouting he said to himself: 'She is done for!' But he ran in plucking his beard and crying: 'Oh, woe is me!' But to himself he said: 'Why didn't I do it sooner?' Aloud he said: 'Alas, what will become of me, poor wretch?' But in his heart: 'What if this traitor isn't dead?' So he went to her, thinking she might be alive, but she was dead" (135). In short, Martínez introduces a degree of psychological complexity unknown to the earlier versions of the tale. Tailoring it to the overall thematic necessities of his work (the condemnation of lust), he creates a sinister, dramatic warning to adulterers—as well as disobedient, stubborn wives.

Although Andreas alludes to the popular biblical story of David and Bathsheba (*Courtly Love*, 200), the variant in the *Whip* is, as we have noted, probably inspired in the *Book of Good Love*. Juan Ruiz tells this tale of adulterous love in two short stanzas. Addressing Master Love, love's allegorical representation, he says:

On account of lust you made David, the prophet,
The one who killed Uriah, send him to war
And place him in the front lines when he said: "Go,
Take this letter to Joab and return."
For the love of Bathsheba, Uriah's wife,
David was a murderer and was delinquent unto God.
Thus, in all his days he never built the temple.
He was forced to do great penance on account of your misdeeds.

(*Feciste por loxuria al profeta David,*
Que mató a Urías, quando l' mandó en la lyd
Poner en los primeros, quando le dixo: "Yd,
Levad esta mi carta a Joab e venid."
Por amor de Berssabe, la muger de Urías,
Fue David omeçida e fizo a Dios fallías;
Non fiz' por ende el tenpro en todos los sus días,
Fizo grand penitençia por las tus maestrías) (stanzas 258–59)

Because of its brevity, Ruiz's version is very much like Capellanus's in his "Rejection of Love." Martínez's, on the other hand, greatly expands the exemplum, providing an in-depth description of the situation and animated portraits of David and Bathsheba. The latter is portrayed as a provocative, calculating temptress:

King David . . . had seen her in her garden every day combing her hair and arraying herself before his eyes, and she came daily to do so, even exposing her breasts, although she pretended that she did not know he was there, as many others are in the habit of doing these days. And so the king, not content with many, loved and coveted the only wife of Uriah, and with her committed carnal sin. . . . Which same he would not have committed had she not desired it when she saw and sensed the beginning of the king's love, and had she not continued to come and array herself as she did. (52–53)

David is clearly shown as the dupe. Impressed with the fact that she has piqued the king's desire, Bathsheba salaciously leads him on while pretending not to notice him. Martínez shows his enthusiasm for his characters, dwelling on King David's vigils and the details of his seduction. The sin of adultery is thus personalized and accorded psychological depth through literary elaboration. And it is only after he has established the characters of David and Bathsheba through this animated and concrete scene that Martínez outlines the disastrous consequences of the illicit union. Furthermore, in his exemplum he details how lust leads not only to adultery and murder, but also to the death of innocents and the violation of the feudal union of sovereign and liege. In other words, he develops, diversifies, and enhances this popular biblical motif, making it more human and emphatically more didactic.

If a comparison were made between the *Whip's* other exempla and their known variants, the situation outlined above would prove to be typical in nearly every instance. That is to say, Martínez draws upon the body of medieval popular tales, never copying, but successfully complicating, dramatizing, and artistically adapting at every step. The didactic folklore of the Middle Ages is accommodated to the theme of his work and continually subordinated to his purpose.

Unlike the majority of his predecessors who utilized the popular tradition in their didactic works, Martínez displays a well-defined artistic concern in his use of tales. It is significant that, although preoccupied with emphasizing the human applications of the lessons taught by the popular tradition, he totally eschews the use of animal fables in the *Whip*. This is because they do not coincide with his realistic vision of the world. Possessing a sober temperament, he chooses to elaborate only those motifs that clearly lend themselves directly to depicting man's folly. The medieval didactic tradition's naive use of animal fables is abandoned for the more concrete, immediate, and dramatic portrayal of the human personality.

Perhaps the most cogent example of this is the tale of the dissolute hermit of Valencia (Part IV). Martínez tells us it is an incident he witnessed with his own eyes; and from the detail and characterization of the episode there is little reason to doubt him. Contrary to his other exempla, which are usually short anecdotes, the hermit's story is by comparison quite long. It possesses a well-structured plot, abounds in dialogue, and is filled with pertinent descriptions. Martínez takes special care to first establish the anchorite's holy reputation, telling how he was revered by the people of the kingdom for his sacrifices, piety, and charity. But while doing so, he provides a revealing description of the man's fine house with its beautiful gardens and his bevy of female Beghards who served him. One day, the holy man contracted with an artist to paint a sacrilegious scene of the crucifixion in a hidden alcove, for he was in reality a hypocrite and a necromancer. Upon completing the scene, the painter felt pangs of conscience and denounced the hermit to the governor of Valencia.

The governor, of course, can scarcely believe the accusation, but decides to investigate it nevertheless. Arriving at the house, he is obsequiously greeted by the hypocritical hermit: "Sir, peace be with you . . . I am gladdened by your visit. What has brought you here? It has been more than two months since you last came to visit this your humble home" (GM, 239). Martínez paints a scene of tremendous irony chronicling the governor's suspicions and the hermit's anxiety as they both walk through the house on an inspection. In the Spartan sleeping quarters the governor asks the reason for the wooden paneling while tapping it. The hermit nervously replies that it was placed there to keep the damp out. The charade is at last abandoned when the governor asks that the door to the hidden alcove behind the wall covering be opened. The anchorite falls to his knees, crossing himself and insisting there is no secret room. Finally, the painter is brought in, and makes a formal accusation in front of witnesses. The alcove is opened and the hermit's hypocrisy exposed. Taken prisoner, he is paraded past a mystified crowd that cannot fathom the justice in arresting such a holy man. The governor must now deal with a public outcry which forces him to publish the unsavory story. Accordingly, the populace is shocked. The hermit is tortured, forced to confess his sins, and finally burned at the stake.

Throughout the story there is a careful delineation of cause and effect, not only of events but of character. We are told how the hermit suddenly pales and is left speechless when the alcove is opened; how the governor dissimulates in his conversation while looking for the right moment to trap the accused; how the righteous painter, feeling he was made a fool of, greets the hermit with bitter sarcasm; and how public opinion changed when confronted with the evidence. The dissolute hermit's tale is not an ordinary exemplum. It is a short story, in that it organizes characters and their thoughts, actions, and interactions into the pattern of a plot. It has a beginning, a climax, and a denouement evoking expectation, suspense, and surprise from the reader. The interest is equally balanced between character and action, while the latter is contrived to test and reveal the former.

The key to Martínez de Toledo's art lies in his capacity to select, elaborate, integrate, animate, and personalize the omnipresent clichés of medieval didactic literature. The *Archpriest of Talavera* is, as we have seen, both traditional and innovative. Philosophically and theologically it is completely orthodox. Artistically, on the other hand, it is revolutionary. On the whole, the work faithfully renders the ideas of its Latin and vernacular models, but improves their presentation through stylistic, thematic, and fictive development. These aspects make it an important link between medieval pedagogical prose and the purely creative, fictional mode of modern literature. In it we witness a crucial point of transition in the rise of the Spanish narrative—we clearly begin to see art's gradual encroachment upon the moral, the domination of the esthetic over the ethical principle. In the *Whip* the craft of fiction begins to subordinate abstraction, and with this we take a giant step toward the creation of the modern novel.

VIII *The Problem of Juan de Ausim*

Any discussion of the sources of the *Archpriest of Talavera* must address itself to the enigma of Juan de Ausim. Martínez states in his prologue that in writing his work he has "gathered together certain notable sayings of a Doctor of Paris, Juan de Ausim by name, who wrote somewhat of the love of God and reprobation of the worldly love of women" (12). Yet all efforts to identify this mysterious figure have been virtually fruitless. In the Toledo 1500 incunabulum "Juan de Ausim" is replaced by "Jean Gerson," a French ecclesiastical statesman (1363–1429) and writer who condemned as immoral Jean de Meung's *Roman de la rose* (*Romance of the Rose*). For this reason, prior to Anna Krause's 1929 study, the search for possible sources was centered upon Gerson's work. It was thought that "Juan de Ausim" was one more of the many careless errors made by Alfonso de Contreras in copying the only extant manuscript of the *Whip*.[46] All comparisons between Martínez and Gerson, however, have proven futile. Amador de los Ríos suggested a possible link with Françesc Eiximenis's *Libro de la donas* (*Book of the Ladies*),[47] but the parallels that exist are much too general; and besides, to derive "Juan de Ausim" from "Françesc Eiximenis" is paleographically impossible.

After von Richthofen confirmed the influence of the *Art of Courtly Love* on the *Whip,* Mario Penna hypothesized that Juan de Ausim was none other than Andreas Capellanus.[48] Nevertheless, the paleographical arguments that purport to equate him to Juan de Ausim are weak. The question of Ausim's identity will probably never be fully resolved. Edwin B. Place, in one of the most cogent arguments thus far, suggests that Contreras's manuscript reads *Juan de Alsim,* making it highly probable that the reference is to the famous thirteenth-century ecclesiastic, Jean Halgrin of Abbeville (ca. 1180–1237), who received his doctorate in 1220 from a Cluniac college at Paris. . . . In 1228, at the request of the king of Aragon, he was sent by Pope Gregory IX to Spain to preach a crusade against the Moors . . . thus becoming well known to Spanish contemporaries. . . . Martínez de Toledo might well have encountered . . . [a] manuscript miscellany headed by Halgrin's work and followed by a reproduction of Book III of Andreas' *De Amore*. As for the paleographical problem involved, *(H)algrin* could easily have been mistaken by a later scribe for *Alsim*: the cursive French miniscule *g* was quite similar to one of the common types of Spanish *s*, the cursive *r* could have been mistaken for *i* and the *in* for *m*.[49]

Place's observations are based on sound paleographical facts, and are especially interesting in light of the close structural, stylistic, and thematic relationship that Parts I and II of the *Whip* bear to medieval preaching, an aspect of the work we will take up in the next chapter.

Raúl A. del Piero has unconvincingly attempted to demonstrate that Juan de Ausim is in reality Nicolaus Auximanus Picenus, a fifteenth-century jurist from the University of Bologna and author of several works of canon law.[50] Basing his conjecture on the graphic likeness of *Auximanus* and *Ausim*, he attempts to prove Martínez's debt to Nicolaus by citing several passages from his *Supplementum Summae Pisanellae* (*Supplement to the Summas of Pisa*). The similarities between the *Whip* and this work, however, are almost exclusively topical. They have as their common source an allusion to Gregory the Great's *Morals on the Book of Job* (Book XXXV), an extremely well-known and often-studied exegesis during the Middle Ages. In fact, this work was so popular that abundant *florilegia* (anthologized selections) of its maxims circulated freely, while many theological compendia also incorporated ideas and references to it.[51] It was considered a theological classic, and there is scarcely a medieval author who was not familiar with Gregory's work.

Although we are not convinced by Mario Penna's paleographical efforts to identify Ausim with Capellanus, on thematic, historical, and other textual grounds (to be discussed in Chapter 5, Section III) we feel the reference is probably to the French chaplain.

CHAPTER 4

The Whip and the Pulpit

THE Iberian Peninsula, like the rest of Europe, witnessed a flowering of sacred oratory during the late Middle Ages. Indeed, some of the greatest medieval preachers called it their homeland: Françesc Eiximenis, Anthony of Padua, Saint Vincent Ferrer, and, most significantly, the founder of the Order of Preachers himself, Saint Dominic. However, it is not until the fifteenth century that, as Juan Beneyto notes, "preaching reaches a singular degree of development" in the peninsula.[1] During this period homiletics attained its artistic and political zenith in the kingdoms of Hispania, and it was in this milieu that Alfonso Martínez conceived and wrote the *Archpriest of Talavera.*

The role of the sermon in the creation of the *Whip* is of fundamental importance, but curiously, scholars have barely touched upon this influence. Erich von Richthofen confirms that the work is a prose tract filled with exempla and tales similar to those found in Jacques de Vitry's sermons and that Martínez uses a "medieval preaching style" as his principal means of expression. Moreover, he concludes that "Jacques de Vitry's work and the works of his successors, Étienne de Bourbon and Alfonso Martínez, are stylistically related," but lamentably does not pursue the matter further.[2] He virtually ignores the extent to which the entire *Whip,* but most especially the first part, is infused with the spirit and methods of the pulpit.

I *The Sermonic Structure of Part I*

Marcelino Menéndez y Pelayo remarks that the first part of the *Archpriest of Talavera* "is a long sermon against lust."[3] Indeed, Part I of the work is a sermon in every sense of the word. It liberally follows, for example, the structural scheme of the medieval university sermon as outlined by the *artes praedicandi* (arts of preaching), while at the same time receiving a strong influence from the less erudite popular preaching of the day. Doubtless recalling the precept that the text of a sacred oration should "be taken from the Bible; be well quoted; have quantity; have quality; be not too short; be not too long; [and] have complete meaning,"[4] Martínez chooses the Great Commandment of Saint Matthew as the theme he develops in his sermon. Matthew 22:37 states: "Thou shalt love the Lord thy God with thy whole heart, and with thy whole soul, and with thy whole mind." Spuriously identifying this as the First Commandment of the Decalogue ("I, the Lord, am your God, who brought you out of the land of Egypt, that place of slavery. You shall not have other gods besides me," Exodus 20:2–3), and not heeding the precept that a text be well quoted, Martínez paraphrases Saint Matthew's Great Commandment and declares the theme of his homily: "Thou shalt love thy God, thy Creator, and thy Lord above all things" (12). It is indeed odd that scholars have not noticed this confusion on Martínez's part and recognized the commentary of the Ten Commandments that subsequently follows as nothing more than a sermonic gloss of this key Apostolic concept. The theme of the love of God was a favorite among the medieval preachers. In fact, the very text the Archpriest paraphrases is considered the model theme for development in the *Arbor Picta de Arte Praedicandi* (*Pictorial Tree of the Art of Preaching*), the "oldest extant visual aid devised for teaching a more effective mode of public speaking."[5]

The classical learned sermon of the Middle Ages calls for the introduction of a *pro-thema* (protheme, or an exordium for the theme itself) after the enunciation of the theme. As Lecoy de la Marche notes, however, its absence is quite common, almost characteristic, in fourteenth- and fifteenth-century popular preaching.[6] Rather than devise a transitional section (protheme) leading to a prayer, Martínez excludes both in the introduction of his sermon and reflects on the gravity and meaning of his chosen text.[7] Nevertheless, Part I of the *Whip* does contain an invocation of divine assistance similar to the prayers of the medieval sermons, although not in the customary position immediately following the thematic declaration. Martínez begins his work with the words: "In the name of the Holy Trinity, Father, Son, and Holy Ghost, three persons and one true God, Maker, Arranger, and Composer of all things, without whom nothing can be well done, well said, begun, half done, or finished, and having as mediator, intercessor, and advocate the humble and spotless Virgin Mary" (11). Von Richthofen rightly calls this a "preaching-prayer formula" and compares it to the invocations of Juan Manuel's *Count Lucanor* and López de Ayala's *Palace Rhymes*.[8] Nevertheless, he fails to recognize that both authors (although in the case of Ayala, no detailed study has been done) received a strong influence from preaching.[9] Martínez's positioning of the customary prayer at the beginning of his work does not gainsay Part I's structural kinship to sacred oratory: Edwin Dargan, for example, describes a type of sermon in which the brief invocation of divine guidance precedes the declaration of the theme.[10]

In the short reflection on the text following its presentation (12–16), Martínez condemns the "dishonest love of women, mad, senseless, and bestial" (15) as the principal force leading to the violation of Saint Matthew's Great Commandment. In this digression he bewails the ways of the world, mentioning some of the vicious manners in which "it is plainly going to ruin" (14). He finishes this by alluding to Matthew 22:37: "And so I will begin by explaining the most important thing, that is, how the love of God is proper love, and none other" (16). This circular detour implicitly confirming the moral validity of his text is identical to one of the methods recommended by Henry of Hesse in his art of preaching: "(1) Let the way of the world be introduced. (2) Let vicious habits be corrected. (3) Let persuasion to the opposite virtue be used. (4) Conclude with the authority from which the digression was made."[11]

The invocation given, the theme stated and confirmed through a declaration of the world's sinful ways, a conclusion derived that leads back to the text, Martínez finishes the introduction of his sermon. We would expect him to proceed to divide, subdivide, and amplify his theme as recommended in the arts of preaching. Martínez, however, only partially complies with these precepts. The university sermons described by the arts of preaching were enormously complex, and could be truly appreciated only by a very learned audience. The assumption of the preaching arts is that their readers are Schoolmen who will wish to sermonize in Latin following rigid formal conventions deemed "artistic." Some of the compendia, nevertheless, allow for flexibility by insisting that the models they describe are not fixed in every detail. Thomas Waleys, for example, comments on the vast diversity of sermon types. Tacitly admitting that his precepts are far from inviolate, he observes that "I find it not only superfluous but impossible to describe the true manners and forms of preaching; especially those used by contemporary preachers. At the moment, it is extremely difficult to find two sermons composed by the same preacher that will wholly conform with each other with regard to their structure."[12] In fact, many such nonconformist sermons have survived. Most of these are in the vernacular and do not follow the structural canons prescribed by the arts in every detail, yet the formal conventions of the learned method of development are perceptible, if somewhat diffuse. These *divisio extra* (lacking divisions) orations were intended to be preached to a mixed audience of clergy and laymen, to please and edify the erudite and the illiterate.[13] Part I of the *Whip* is very similar to such sermons, borrowing the general principle of structure from the medieval art of preaching but neglecting a strict adhesion to the paradigm of the university method (*divisio intra*, or with divisions).

Rather than depending on some hairsplitting word-for-word division in the amplification of his sermon, the body of Martínez's composition is made up of independent meditations (divisions, if liberally interpreted) that are closely and constantly related to his main theme.[14] Within this broader, less demanding structure he interweaves subthemes that involve frequent repetition of the same words and ideas. Each of these is intimately tied to and aimed at proving the righteousness of his text. As in musical variations, the theme of Part I is first stated and then followed by multiple, differing restatements. The general structural principle of this sermon, and indeed those described in the arts, is much like a symphony, varying some feature of a harmonized theme while retaining enough of its identity to preserve a relationship with the original declaration.[15]

Chapters I–XVIII in Part I of the *Whip* are all primary variations on the Great Commandment of Saint Matthew. While space does not permit a full analysis of every one of these variants, the thematic concordance of a few sections will illustrate the point. During our survey it should be noticed that each of the chapters in Part I is a self-contained dialectically structured variation and proof of Matthew 22:37.

The first chapter corroborates our premise. Its title alone is enough to show that it is a variant restatement and gloss of Martínez's theme: "How he who madly loves is displeasing God" (19). In a syllogistic manner, our author proposes the thesis of this variation: "First I will state a proposition that no one can gainsay, to wit, that no man can be pleasing to God who gives himself up to worldly love" (*ibid.*). He authorizes his premise by declaring that fornication is condemned in the Old and New Testaments and asserting that God "commands the punishment of all those who are guilty of fornication and lechery" (*ibid.*). The antithesis of the argument is represented in the "vile, obscene, and horrible acts of lechery committed in sundry forms" (*ibid.*). Continuously organizing along a dialectical pattern, he attempts to persuade by affirming that "if Our Lord God had desired that this sin . . . might be committed without sin, He would not have ordained the celebration of marriage, for it is clear and plain that people would multiply more rapidly by committing fornication than otherwise" (20). Then, aiming at the emotional appeal for his reader, he adduces one of the favorite topics of medieval preaching, the Passion of Christ.[16] Following this, the synthesis of the argument is reached: "Let him who can or will, therefore, bear in mind that only the love of God is true love, since He died for love of you. And then you would repay Him by loving another!" (*ibid.*). Not surprisingly, the conclusion Martínez derives from his disputation is none other than a variant rephrasing of his initial theme.

Chapter IX, as would be expected, follows this same analytical structure, repeating words and ideas similar to those of the section just examined. In it, the Archpriest sets out to prove

"How love causes many to perjure themselves and commit crimes" (33). Announcing the thesis of this chapter, he declares: "There is another reason why love is properly condemned by those who rightly reflect upon it. In the world there is no evil or crime which does not arise from it, for, as I have said, murders, adulteries, and lies have their source in love, for the lover often commits them in order to please or deceive his mistress, since his vows are not properly to be called vows, but rather lies" (33–34). The moral antithesis of this statement is symbolized by a brief exemplification of the "husband secretly stealing from his wife in order to regale his mistress, giving her bad days, bad breakfasts, and bad suppers" (34). Martínez then tells us of the "beatings and kickings and cuffings" the wife must bear as a result of her husband's misdirected love. Aware of the dialectical arrangement of his argument, he synthesizes it in a manner strongly reminiscent of Scholastic disquisition: "In sum [the Spanish original reads *Suma:*], all evils have their origin in dishonest love" (*ibid.*). The consequence of errant love confirmed, he alludes to the First Commandment of the Decalogue and restates the unifying theme of his sermon: "Fly, therefore, the love of those from whom so many evils proceed, and love God who is the source of all good" (35).

The Archpriest's insistence on methodical, indeed deliberate, concatenation of ideas, much as in the medieval university sermon, is evident throughout the first part of the *Whip*. In the chapter just discussed, for instance, the recurrence of words and phrases like *therefore*, *behold*, *the aforesaid*, *in sum*, *I'll tell you more*, and so on, betrays the preacher's affinity for logical argumentation and attests to the conscious control he maintains over his exposition. Dialectic and rhetoric, hence, merge in the first part of the work to form a structure and language whose goal is identical to the sermon's: moral persuasion.

If lust, according to our examples, is shown to displease God, cause mendacity and criminal behavior, in short, violate His Great Commandment, it also induces some very prosaic and somewhat comical consequences from our modern point of view. In Chapter XVI, Martínez exemplifies "how he who gives himself to lechery loses strength" (48). The authorities and arguments against concupiscence in this section are similar to those found in Chapter III, "On Lust," of the *Espéculo de los legos* (*Mirror of the Laymen*), a fifteenth-century Castilian translation of the *Speculum Laicorum* (*Layman's Mirror*), a manual of exempla and arguments for preachers.[17] Far more analytical than the anonymous clerk who composed the *Mirror*, however, Martínez clearly delineates a cause and effect relationship between lust and the weakening of physical strength. As is customary in the structure of the chapters in Part I, he declares his new thesis and gives examples demonstrating how "men . . . are made weak in four ways" (*ibid.*). These proofs, as in the sections already studied, arrive at a predictable conclusion, a variant restatement of the text of his sermon: "Therefore, since unbridled love is the cause of so many bodily ills, it would be the part of wisdom to abandon it and give it no importance, although at times, to be sure, holding things to be of no importance is the source of much harm and confusion, for he who turns his back upon his enemy, dies at his hands. So then, for God's sake let us truly love in such wise, loving God alone, that we shall gain everlasting life" (50).

The three representative chapters examined from Part I of the work are systematically constructed primary variations and proofs of Matthew 22:37. The fundamental structure of the first part of the *Whip* is, accordingly, a spiraling arrangement which makes continuous contrapuntal reference to a central idea, the text of the homily. Although Martínez does not follow the recommendation of the arts of preaching to divide his theme into its component parts and words to facilitate exegesis, he nevertheless pursues the orderly, circuitous exposition characteristic of the pulpit.[18]

At the end of Chapter XVIII, the Archpriest reaches a transitional point in the overall corpus of Part I. At this juncture he departs from the primary variations of the initial eighteen chapters and moves on to a secondary and subordinate group. Much like a *codetta*, to again use the musical analogy, this passage marks a turning point in the development of the theme: "Hitherto I have spoken of disorderly love and how it should be shunned, and how we should love only God. I will continue now by showing that he who loves transgresses the Ten Commandments and commits all seven deadly sins, whence all evil arises" (61). This technique of ending a section of thematic variations while at the same time preparing the audience (in the *Whip*'s case, the reader) for further, though secondary, development of the central idea is quite common in pulpit oratory and indicative of the rhetorical care with which sermons were composed.[19]

Chapter XIX serves as the introduction to a new unit of variations on Matthew 22:37 which Martínez intends to add to the remainder of his amplification. In it, he projects the orderly scheme he will follow in the ensuing eighteen chapters: "First I say to you that he who practices, and continues to practice, dishonest love, just to indulge his unbridled appetite, this fellow, I say, transgresses one after the other all the commandments of God. Furthermore, he commits the seven deadly sins, annuls the powers of the spirit, destroys the five senses, corrupts the seven virtues (the four cardinal virtues as well as the three theological ones), and neglects to practice the seven works of mercy" (61–62). The trajectory of the rest of the sermon having been subdivided in this manner, Martínez begins a methodical gloss of the Decalogue and the virtues enumerated.[20]

Chapter XX repeats the chosen text for the homily and again erroneously identifies it as "the first commandment" (62). However, the confusion here between Matthew 22:37 and Exodus 20:2–3 is incidental. What is significant is that this chapter, the capstone for a new set of variations, reiterates the unifying theme of the entire sermon: "Thou shalt love thy God above all things" (*ibid.*). This emphatic restatement of the text opens the way for a new set of repetitions and proofs of how Saint Matthew's Great Commandment, along with the Decalogue and the Christian virtues, is violated by "disordered love" (*amor desordenado*).

With the heterogenous repetitions and verifications of the text following its latest restatement, the structure of Part I becomes increasingly complex. Much like the subdivisions of the university sermon, several of the sections in this new unit of tautologies are variations on the variations found in Chapters I–XVIII. For example, Chapter XXII is a gloss of the Fourth Commandment ("Honor your father and your mother, that you may have a long life in the land in which the Lord, your God, is giving you," Exodus 20:12). This is a clear structural allusion to Chapter V, "How he who loves hates his father and mother, his kin and friends" (27). The same is true of Chapter XXIV, the Fifth Commandment ("You shall not kill," Exodus 20:13), and Chapters III and XIV ("How love is the cause of death, violence, and war" [22], and "How love is the cause of deaths and other evils" [42]). Chapter XXVII, the Eighth Commandment ("You shall not bear false witness against your neighbor," Exodus 20:16), is essentially a varying repetition of Chapter IX, "How love causes many to perjure themselves and commit crimes" (33). This concentric, spiraling thematic concordance is evident throughout when the primary variations (Chapters I–XVIII) of the theme are compared to its secondary variations (Chapters XX–XXIX).

In Chapters XX–XXIX, Martínez demonstrates how misguided love transgresses the commandments of the Decalogue, and how in turn it is diametrically at odds with the Great Commandment. Although Part I of the *Whip* may appear to be quite amorphous at first reading, when examined in the light of preaching structure a definite thematic organization can be perceived. It proceeds with a sweeping circling motion that constantly brings it back to the theme of the unquestioned love of God. Again and again, each succeeding chapter repeats and confirms, either directly or indirectly, the necessity of loving God above all else.

At the end of the gloss of the Tenth Commandment (Chapter XXIX), the Archpriest reaches another juncture, or *codetta*, in which he concludes that "mad love is the source of all evil" (77). As in the transition from primary to secondary variations, he announces further thematic divisions: "further, that love is the cause of committing the seven deadly sins, for there is not a single one which is not committed by lovers as you will see below" (*ibid.*).[21] As a true preacher, Martínez once again projects the remaining course of his sermon and reveals his awareness of a systematic method of theme development.

As he proved that all of the Ten Commandments are violated

by disordered love, Martínez, in Chapters XXX-XXXVI, demonstrates how the misled lover commits the seven deadly sins. Characteristically, these new tertiary variations are implicit confirmations of the righteousness of his text. Significantly, every succeeding unit of variations (primary, secondary, and tertiary) becomes shorter as the end of the sermon draws near. For example, a fourth group ("How he who loves loses all the virtues") is developed within the space of one chapter (XXXVII). In it, Martínez adduces the various arguments on how the seven virtues are unattainable for the earthly lover. In the beginning and middle of Part I, he devotes entire chapters to proving one thesis. Toward the end of the homily, however, he demonstrates several points under one heading. Superficially, this progressive diminution of arguments seems to lack a reason and appears to be a structural fault lending an asymmetrical configuration to the first part. Nevertheless, as with all the formal elements in Part I discussed up until now, this "flaw" does indeed have a reason and a precedent: pulpit oratory. There is a subtle psychology to medieval sermon composition. To avoid boring their audience, the preachers generally constructed their orations so that their pace quickened, presenting a greater variety of new materials near the end of the discourse.[22]

The closing of Martínez's sermon comes at the end of Chapter XXXVII with the *amen* (97) typical of medieval homiletics. The variations of his theme have been adduced, argued, and proven. The sermon *per se* is finished. However, "the preacher can make a practical recapitulation of his sermon, so that if the hearers have not attended the beginning, they may know on what the sermon is effectively based."[23] Indeed, it would seem the Archpriest did just this in the final chapter of Part I, for its title reads: "Conclusion: How all evil proceeds from love" (*ibid.*). Nevertheless, its content does not correspond to its heading. This is readily explainable, since Part I was doubtless written some time before the remainder of the tract and its last chapter altered to form a transition between it and the later material.[24]

Accordingly, the first part of the *Archpriest of Talavera* has every structural indication of being a sermon. Although it does not strictly follow the formal conventions of the university method, considered in its entirety it is developed along the lines of the art of preaching. Lecoy de la Marche describes a popular sermon design similar to the one followed by Martínez in that it is based on dialectical argumentation: "It consists of considering two opposite propositions, in adopting one and rejecting the other. . . . This type of argument deals, above all, with morality, good and evil, that that is to be sought after and that that is to be eschewed."[25] With its advocacy of the love of God and the rejection of lust, Part I of the *Whip* clearly fits this description.

The canons of composition we have outlined above serve to interpret the first part of the *Whip* under a new light and lead to a better and more detailed understanding of the entire work. The medieval art of preaching succinctly explains Part I's sometimes bewildering transitions, its rapid changes of direction, and its recurrent repetition of themes. Each of its chapters has its preordained function and an intimate structural relation to a central idea: all reasons, arguments, and proofs are tightly bound to the moral righteousness of Saint Matthew's Great Commandment. Martínez was well aware that, as Saint Vincent Ferrer says, "preaching is comparable to a textile: if you pull one thread of the warp all the others follow. Thus, a sermon should be woven: one example tied to the next, one authority to the following authority, and everything should refer to the theme, if it is a well ordered oration."[26]

II *Preaching and Aspects of the* Whip's *Style*

In addition to the deliberate sermonic structure of the first part of the *Whip*, all four parts of the work bear strong traces of the themes, motifs, diction, and style of medieval preaching. Erich von Richthofen recognizes an inherent tension between a latinizing impulse (hyperbaton, periodic sentence structure, neologism, etc.) and a "folksy element" in the *Whip*'s style, but, believing this unusual contraposition to be unconscious on our author's part, he is somewhat at a loss to explain it.[27] The German scholar fails to analyze Martínez's peculiar mode of expression in light of the preaching tradition.

Martínez's style in the *Whip* possesses an internal logic all its own. The two modes, erudite and popular, are in fact deliberate elements of our author's unique style. The motivating force behind this at first paradoxical verbal dialectic is, we believe, rooted in the preacher's desire to appeal to a diverse audience. In his study of the Valencian sermons of Saint Vincent Ferrer, Roque Chabás observes that the mixture of the cultivated with the profane is an integral note of preaching stylistics; while Homer G. Pfander, referring to the medieval popular sermon in England, even points out instances where orations were not conducted at all times entirely in English, but partially in Latin.[28] The peasantry of medieval England, of course, had little familiarity with Latin. According to Pfander, the reason for this linguistic mixture is that "the uncultivated minds [in the audience] were impressed just as much in the late Middle Ages as today by hearing what they could only partially understand."[29] Indeed, linguistic and stylistic contrast is common to works within the preaching tradition, and certainly not alien to Castilian fifteenth-century homiletics, as shown by J. Rodríguez-Puértolas's study of the poet-preacher Iñigo de Mendoza.[30]

Throughout the *Archpriest of Talavera* the deliberate fusion of Scholastic and colloquial diction predominates, creating a style in many respects identical to that of the medieval sermon. Although the popular element understandably holds sway in the dialogues of its exempla, it also appears in the most cultivated, strictly narrative, parts of the work. Latinate neologisms and syntax coexist with the grossest expressions and malapropisms; and Scholastic arguments are frequently authorized with a rustic proverb. For example, the passage reproving lechery at the end of Part I:

> [The lecher] can no longer exercise the seven virtues: faith, hope, charity, prudence, temperance, fortitude, and justice, and thus he is turned into an irrational beast. Worse, the vile act of lechery causes the wretch to become callous in sin, not only in this one but in others by contamination, and he grows old in them. Many, therefore, are damned who die suddenly when they least expect it or think they are secure, and they say: "Today or tomorrow I will mend my way, or get rid of such and such a vice." Thus by putting things off from day to day the poor wretch ends in the arms of Satan, which is the worst fate of all, it is needless to say. (24–25)

([*El lujurioso*] *de las syete virtudes non puede usar: fee, esperança, caridad, prudencia, temprança, fortaleza, justiçia, asý que es fecho como bestia yrracional; e lo peor, quel aucto vil, luxurioso, fase al cuytado del onbre adormir en los pecados, asý en aquél como en los otros por comitançia, e en ellos por grand tienpo envejeçer. Por do muchos son fallados dañapdos que mueren subitamente quando non piensan, o más seguros están, diziendo: "Oy, mañana, me henmendaré; de tal viçio me quitaré."* (GM, 52)

In this passage the Scholastic conception of the seven virtues and seven deadly sins, as well as learned diction and syntax, appear side by side with popular proverbs and idioms. Indeed, to appreciate the extent to which this intermixing of seemingly antagonistic elements is carried out, one need only open the *Whip* at random. Hyperbatons are followed by straightforward, simple, even vulgar, constructions. Scriptural citations and allusions to Latin tracts appear with the most commonplace proverbial endorsement. Theologically complex dissertations on subjects such as freedom of choice and judicial astrology are punctuated by outbursts of barbarisms, folksy commentary, and exempla.

The symbiosis of the popular and erudite is very conscious on Martínez's part, reflecting the careful psychology of audiences practiced by medieval preachers. A man familiar with pulpit oratory, he employed its style in writing his work because his aim was principally pedagogic—the dissemination of the Word to the greatest number of people at any given instance. It must not be forgotten that the *Whip*, despite the fact that it contains some of the most amusing and ribald scenes in early Spanish literature, is an orthodox tract reproving worldly love. The one vehicle best suited for accomplishing this objective was the heterogeneous style of the medieval sermon. Through it, two quite disparate audiences are reached by combining the indecorous with the learned, giving rise to a unique form of expression that, as Erich Auerbach remarks, "impresses the taste of later ages as grotesque."[31]

With this in mind, we can proceed to look more closely at the particulars of Martínez's style and point out analogies in contemporary preaching. Through comparison with some of Saint Vincent Ferrer's sermons, and reference to several arts of preaching, the *Whip*'s stylistic kinship to pulpit oratory becomes increasingly clear.

Von Richthofen notices that exclamations are often used in the work in order to elicit an emotional response from the reader.[32] Turning to Françesc Eiximenis's *Ars Praedicandi* (*Art of Preaching*), we see that the Franciscan identifies a "fervent voice" with the sermon's task of persuasion.[33] Similarly, Henry of Hesse even more specifically counsels the use of an exclamatory style and declares that "exclamation should be made by *Oh* in exhorting, and *Alas* in correcting."[34] Comparing the heated interjections of the *Whip* with those in Vincent Ferrer's Valencian sermons, we find they are identical. Martínez's frequent *oh*'s (*yuy*), *ah*'s (*ay*), and *alas*es (*o*) are the same *oh*'s (*ooy*), *ah*'s (*ay*), and *alas*es (*oo*) used by Ferrer,[35] and nothing more than oratorical colors of the art of preaching that serve, according to Fray Martín de Córdoba, to capture the favor and attention of an audience.[36]

Another favorite stylistic device of the preachers in achieving the emotional involvement of their audience was the rhetorical question, a method Fray Martín identifies as the fourth essential way of developing a sermon,[37] and an artifice recommended by Saint Augustine in his *First Catechetical Instruction*.[38] Martínez and Vincent Ferrer use it abundantly, and its utilization in the former can be, we believe, attributed directly to pulpit oratory:

Martínez: Tell me, my friend, how many have you seen or heard of who loved in this world whose life was not made up of pain and suffering, worry, sighs, and vexations, sleeplessness, lying awake all night, lack of appetite, fretting, and, even worse, many of them dying of this evil and others going mad, and if they die their souls go to everlasting torment, not to mention their corporeal pain and suffering for two, three, or twenty years? (31)
Ferrer: Tell me, good man, do you have a son? And what do you give him? Can't you see that that is improper? . . . Is there anyone here who upon seeing the sun rise says to it: "Welcome, sun, give us the grace that we might have much hay, much fruit, and many vines?" Oh, idolatry! And you worship the sun? (Chabás, IX, 86–87)

The use of questions and fervent interjections by the preacher was a fundamental characteristic of his pedagogical art. The need to maintain the undivided attention of his public caused him to use these tonal variations and was, as Lecoy de la Marche notes, one of the most salient stylistic aspects of medieval sacred oratory. Many times a preacher would alter the narrative course of his sermon and "pose questions to the people."[39] Furthermore, the question and exclamation are ideal persuasive tropes, for they are more accusatory than anything else and must have elicited a pious, even remorseful, reaction from audiences. Preachers were not beyond browbeating the faithful in order to convince.

The familiar quality of exchange, the seeming intimacy of question and answer in personal, often colloquial, diction is one of the *Whip*'s stylistic graces. The artifice serves to break down the barrier between author and reader, to bridge the narrative gulf and thus persuade more effectively. Martínez was doubtless aware that the verbal instrument most propitious for accomplishing this and conveying his lesson was the language and style of pulpit oratory—a mode whose methods had been well proven in over fourteen centuries of Christian homiletics. Although the Archpriest was a highly educated man privy to Scholastic learning, while writing his didactic masterpiece he knew full well the validity of Vincent Ferrer's admonition: "In preaching or exhorting use simple and domestic diction, and be sure to be precise."[40]

Throughout the *Whip*, *occupatio* (or what von Richthofen calls *brevitas*) formulae are used continuously.[41] At many points in the narrative, Martínez refuses to reveal what he might say, or to adduce exempla that could further elucidate the particular thesis he is explaining. Adopting a posture of feigned modesty, he often tells us, when finishing an exemplum substantiating the moral of his arguments, that he knows of so many similar illustrations "that it would be quite impossible to describe them, so many and varied are they" (30). In order to avoid trying his reader's patience with excessive anecdotes and to win his favor through promised brevity, he notes that "I could say a great deal more . . . but shall refrain lest I bore you with my longwindedness" (79), although "I could tell you of a thousand cases like these" (137). While this rhetorical maneuver is common in literature dating back to classical times, it is a pronounced feature of medieval sermonics also. When a preacher reached a juncture in his discourse, he would take leave of his subject by using one of these tropes. His reason for utilizing them was principally psychological. Through them he reassured his audience that he was in total command of his material, and in fact knew much more about it than he wished to reveal. In other words, he tacitly affirms that the lesson of his example is present throughout nature, righteous, and indeed universal. Although a commonplace in the history of literature, the use of *occupatio* in Martínez's work was doubtless intensified and conditioned by his familiarity with pulpit rhetoric. These closing formulae, as well as the formulaic exemplum incipits *Yten* ("Item," in its admonitory sense), *rregla es* ("It is the rule"), *común rregla es* ("it is a well-known rule"), *contarte he un enxiemplo* ("I will tell you an exemplum"), *paren mientes a este enxiemplo* ("pay attention to this example"), are present in the sermons of Ferrer and considered a rhetorical outgrowth of the medieval art of preaching by J. Th. Welter in his *L'Exemplum dans la littérature religieuse et didactique du moyen age.*[42]

The Archpriest frequently uses extended enumerations to adorn and emphasize his descriptions. In numerous passages of his work there are veritable grotesque accumulations of basically synonymous objects, verbs, nouns, and adjectives. In these verbal torrents he reaches colorful high points of style in which, as Dámaso Alonso observes, "two idiomatic forms of plenty come together: that of popular expression, which tends to particularize; and that of the moralist who offers a series of alternatives in order that his doctrine might be more universal."[43] They mirror the preacher's obsession with the universality, yet individual applicability, of his lesson, and are, from the strictly stylistic point of view, a manifestation of sermonic amplification. The sacred orator's principal contribution to a sermon consists, in the words of Harry Caplan, "in his treatment of sermon-*dilatatio.*"[44] A fundamental device recommended by the arts of preaching for the distension of ideas is the *adnomimatio* ("naming"), or enumerations and the multiplication of synonyms.[45]

Martínez avails himself of this technique, for example, when he tells us of men driven mad by lust. Their lives are "pain and suffering, worry, sighs, and vexations, sleeplessness, lying awake all night, lack of appetite, fretting, and even worse, many of them dying of the evil" (31). Later when speaking of man's desire to escape Fortune, he bombards his reader with the "popes, cardinals, patriarchs, archbishops, bishops, abbots, doctors, masters in theology, in law and canons, mortared doctors like Augustine, Ambrose, Isidore, Leander, Jerome, Bernard, Anselm, Bede, Crisostome, Dionysius" (GM, 261) and myriad other learned men who turned their back stoically on the mutable lady.

Looking to Saint Vincent Ferrer's sermons, we see identical accumulations of like, or nearly alike, objects and actions. In one sermon he mocks the "poverty" of some laborers:

> Now see here, do you have fields and olive groves? Do you see poverty in this? This that requires seed, workers, cutters, carriers, and wagons to take the wheat to where it is prepared? Alas, such poverty! Do you have vines—by God!—you need diggers, basins, men to wash the basins, porters, and presses. Oh, on my life, such poverty! Do you have sheep? Then you have shepherds, dogs, feed, flower, etcetera. Alas, such poverty! Oh, such poverty you must bear! Mules, horses, stables, stableboys, hay, oats, etc. . . . (Chabás, VII, 139)

Repetitive enumerations are, then, an integral component of medieval sermonic rhetoric, and in Dámaso Alonso's words, "the most salient stylistic aspect in the Archpriest of Talavera."[46]

The prolixity of Martínez's style is closely linked to the medieval preacher's impulse to accumulate, repeat, and hence paradoxically particularize. However, the preaching ornaments we have encountered in the *Whip* are not mere empty rhetoric, but an attempt to amplify ideas as well—to exemplify in as many ways as possible the Christian tenets underlying the work. In the *Archpriest of Talavera*'s case, as we have seen, this is the unique distinction between divine and human love. What appears to be verbal excess in his masterpiece is specifically motivated by the preacher's conscious endeavor to "dot every *i*," as Jacques de Vitry puts it. Repetition is forgivable, indeed desirable, so that the lesson might be clearly understood and persuasive.[47] The pulpit's reliance on rhetoric is a direct result of its didactic goal: the need to profoundly, minutely, yet effectively, express the sometimes difficult Christian ethic and inspire an audience to virtuous action. The preachers' and Martínez's cultivation of style was an immediate consequence of its useful, pragmatic, docent possibilities.

A particularly effective verbal stratagem used in medieval sermons is the weaving of rhyming lines into the narrative. The rhymed phrases served a mnemonic purpose for the preacher, and often, because of their prosodic quality, sounded proverbial even if they were not. Thus, they were left impressed on the minds of the public long after the oration was over. Pérez Pastor in 1901 was the first to comment upon Martínez's "fondness for rhymed prose," and von Richthofen later observed that "Alfonso Martínez has a propensity to use consonant and assonant rhyme."[48] Both scholars, however, fail to note that rhymed narrative is a constant in homiletic literature dating back to the time of Saint Augustine.[49] Particularly when emphasizing a point or passing moral judgment, the Archpriest rhymes his exclamations: "Oh cruel judgment, how little considered and less pondered" (20) (*¡O Juyzio cruel, poco pensado, menos cogitado!*); "Alas, Virgin Mary, how can one see such a thing and not burst with rage" (104) (*¡Ay, virgen María, como non rrebyenta quien vee tal sobrevienta!*); "and since up to this point I have reproved the love of women, it would not be fitting for me to praise the love of men" (164) (*e porque fasta aquí el amor de las mugeres fue rreprovado, conviene quel amor de los onbres non sea loado*). In his study of the popular sermon, Pfander declares that the preachers made use of rhyme "to serve two main purposes: first, to mark the structural divisions of the sermon by stating Text, Principals, Subdivisions, and Closing; and second, to supply dialation and ornament."[50] In Martínez's work rhyme appears most frequently when he departs from his Latin sources,[51] and hence also performs a distinctive structural function. The Archpriest's predilection for rhymed narrative is, then, not so much an individual stylistic trait as one more trace of pulpit oratory in his work. Doubtless exploiting the didactic possibilities of rhythmic prose, he endows a paroemiological air to his pronouncements. When no longer following the authority of his Latin models, he feels compelled to impart conclusiveness to his voice by admonishing in a style reminiscent of the popular proverb.

Turning to what seems the most outstanding stylistic contribution of the *Whip* to early Spanish prose, we must now consider the relationship of the rapid, direct dialogues and monologues of the characters in its exempla to pulpit techniques. Menéndez y Pelayo perceptively remarks that Martínez "had a high degree of dramatic instinct, a sense of the more intense side of life, and he managed to divine the rhythm of dialogue."[52] While this is doubtless so, it is equally true that dialogic exempla occasionally as dramatic as his were the natural outgrowth of the sermon tradition. The Abbé Bourgain, one of the early students of medieval French sermons, asserts that dialogue constitutes a type of preaching unto itself authorized by frequent use and reserved mostly for stirring effects.[53] Indeed, when reading the sermons of an accomplished preacher like Vincent Ferrer, it is easy to imagine him reciting the dialogues in his anecdotes with all the appropriate facial expressions and gestures in order to move even the most recalcitrant audience:

Pay attention . . . there once was a great and good master of theology, a very accomplished preacher, so much so in fact that people would come from all around to hear and marvel at him. One day he had just preached an especially devout sermon, and as he was getting down from the pulpit, an old woman said to him: "Oh, master, give me your holy hand so I can kiss it." Seeing her piety and devotion, the master gave her his hand. When she got hold of it, she kissed it and said: "Blessed was the day you were born; God shone His grace upon me when I baptized you!" The master retorted: "What did you say?" "Oh, I baptized you. When your mother gave birth to you you were all blue and everyone thought you'd die and therefore I baptized you." The master said: "And tell me the way you baptized me. Do you remember?" "Do I remember! Oh, sir, I've only baptized once in these hundred years of mine. Do I remember!" And the master said: "Tell me the manner in which you baptized me." "Gladly. When you were born, we thought you would die, so I took some water in a bowl, or some other container, and sprinkled it on you saying 'I baptize you in the name of the

Holy Trinity and the Virgin Mary and Saint Michael and all the celestial court.' " "Oh, woe is me! I'm not a Christian!" said the master. "That isn't the way you're supposed to baptize." Finally, he had himself properly baptized, took his vows anew, and started all over again from the beginning. (Chabás, VIII, 42–43)

The preacher employs dialogues to make the characters in his exempla come alive, gain the attention of his audience, remove his lesson from the realm of abstraction, and simplify it.

As in the medieval homilies, the anecdotes in the *Whip* are usually introduced by a general statement followed by the concrete, or particularized, example of the abstraction. In the best pulpit tradition, moreover, Martínez usually explores the humorous possibilities of the stories through the use of hyperbolic language that tends to characterize the situation and the people they portray. Most of the tales are developed through dramatic means. Like Ferrer and a host of other preachers, the Archpriest often lets individuals engaged in heated dialogue act out the moral he wishes to convey. Expounding on a favorite theme of the pulpit, the disobedience of wives, for example, he re-creates the conversation of a man and his wife on pilgrimage:

Another wife was going on pilgrimage with her husband. They sat down in the shade of a poplar tree and, while they were resting, a thrush burst into song, and the husband said: "God bless you! Do you hear, wife, how the thrush is singing?" And she replied: "But don't you see by its feathers and its small head that it's not a thrush but a throstle?" Said the husband: "You fool! Don't you see by the color of its neck and its long tail that it's a thrush and nothing but a thrush?" But she said: "And don't you see by its song and the way it wags its head that it can't be anything but a throstle?" Said the husband: "Go to the devil, you pigheaded idiot! It's a thrush!" His wife answered: "By God and my soul, I say it's a throstle." Then said the husband: "The devil must have brought that thrush here!" And she replied: "By the Virgin Mary, it's a throstle!" Then the husband, in a rage, took the stick he used on the donkey and broke her arm with it, so, instead of going on a pilgrimage to pray to Saint Mary to give them the son they wanted, they returned to a hermitage to pray to Saint Anthony to heal the stupid woman's arm she had broken by arguing. (137)

The similarity in use and structure of dialogue in medieval sacred oratory and in the *Archpriest of Talavera* is self-evident. The re-creation of direct, active speech in both sermons and Martínez's work is used as a satirico-didactic vehicle to undermine the morally reprehensible and frequently unorthodox behavior of people. In creating his vivid exempla, Martínez surely looked to the pulpit for stylistic and formal guidelines. The dramatic tales of the popular preachers afforded him models worthy of imitation, full of the simple, if sometimes exasperating, facts of daily life. Direct, forceful, and candid, their dramatic exempla frequently went beyond the proportions of narrative dialogue and, like those of Martínez, approached the theatrical in intensity and diversity. As the Abbé Bourgain remarks, in the great majority of sermonic tales "there are numerous characters. One might say that they come and go, enter and exit, as if in a play. There is considerable staging, a lively representation with intrigues and a denouement."[54]

III *The Forbidden Fruit*

Apart from the *Whip*'s stylistic and structural kinship to the medieval sermon, its main thematic inspiration and direction also stem from the same source. The text that Martínez sermonically glosses in Part I was, as we have noted, a favorite with preachers, while the reprobation of lust is a theme as old as the preaching tradition itself.[55] Another very specific attitude, however, stands out in Martínez's relation to the medieval pulpit: his disparagement of woman.

While the *Whip* owes an enormous debt to the *Fates of Illustrious Men* and the *Art of Courtly Love* (two works sharing antifeminist tendencies), neither of these so openly, exuberantly, and insistently maligns women as the Castilian masterpiece does. In form and content, Martínez's misogynistic leanings bear a stronger resemblance to those we find in the popular sermon. Since the time of Saint Paul, a negative opinion of women has played a fundamental role in Christian homiletics. Moreover, during the low Middle Ages the vilification of females was considered almost the exclusive province of the clergy. Chaucer's Wife of Bath, for example, alludes to the popular denigration of women by churchmen. Attacking the Clerk, she turns and says: "For trusteth wel, it is an impossible / That any clerk wol speken good of wyves, / But-if it be of holy seintes lyves, / Ne of noon other womman never the mo."[56] Corroborating the Wife of Bath's indictment, G. R. Owst notes that "it is woman *par excellence* . . . that calls down the full fury of the . . . preachers in satire and complaint."[57] In the sermons of the later Middle Ages woman was often pictured as the gateway to hell, the personification of lust, vanity, pride, the seven deadly sins, the promoter of all earthly evils: indeed, the very role imputed to her in the *Archpriest of Talavera*.[58]

A few excerpts from some late medieval homilies will confirm their intimate thematic ties with the *Whip*. A Spaniard and a paragon of preachers, Saint Vincent Ferrer, for instance, denounces women for their stubbornness in a tone and manner more than reminiscent of Martínez de Toledo's:

And when God created woman what did he say? "I will give man a helpmate," although He should have said "I will give him the instrument of his destruction." What do I mean by this? . . . Well, here's an example. If a woman wants a new dress, she taunts her husband from matins till vespers: "Sir, a new dress for me, a new robe . . . please, please. The ones I have are no good . . ." Bla, bla, bla. She doesn't leave the poor wretch in peace. He objects: "But I have no money, dear." She replies: "Get me one," and so on, until he must borrow money to buy it for her. (Chabás, VIII, 293)

The garrulous woman in the *Whip* anxious to know her husband's secret is even more insistent. Using the same vehicle of direct speech, Martínez portrays her obstinacy in extracting the confidence from her spouse:

"Tell me, now; tell me, won't you?" This with embraces, flattery, kisses, and when she has exhausted this vein she will say: "Don't drive me frantic! . . . You're killing me! Don't upset my stomach! . . . For God's sake tell me! Wretch that I am, miserable and unlucky! Oh, what a lump you are! Why do you act like that? Oh, what a boor! I'll have something to say about this! Tell me now, for God's sake, by my soul and body! Well, if you won't, I give you my word that I'll never speak to you again! Won't you, won't you, won't you tell me?" And at the third "won't you" she will say: "Oh, go away and leave me in peace!" And she lifts her eyebrows and squats on the ground, her hand on her cheek, morose and even weeping with rage, red as a pomegranate, sweating like a galley slave, her heart pounding like that of a lioness, while she gnaws her lips and stares fiercely at you. If you speak to her she will refuse to answer; if you touch her she will turn her back, saying: "Get out! I know how you love me! I believed you once and I've regretted it ever since!" Then she will pretend to sigh, although she has no desire to. Then, perhaps, the poor spiritless nincompoop will say: "Don't be angry, I'll tell you." (131–32)

No mean psychologist Martínez, his exemplum depicting feminine stubbornness is far more perceptive of character than Ferrer's, but the theme, motif, and method are the same.

Another favorite preaching theme is feminine vanity. As Lecoy de la Marche declares, it "is one of woman's defects for which the preachers never lose zest. They shower all their bile and rancor upon it."[59] Vincent Ferrer particularly condemns her use of ostentatious clothes, jewelry, and cosmetics as a symbol of frivolous and sinful conceit (see Chabás, VIII, 295). Likewise, Martínez takes great pleasure in implicitly condemning feminine vainglory while rummaging through a typical woman's chest, in which she keeps the objects catering to the whims of her pride:

Here you will find mother-of-pearl, there rings, here earrings, there bracelets, many wimples lined with silk, scarves, flounces, three or four lined kerchiefs, richly embroidered cambrics, Catalan toques, headdresses covered with silver work, . . . sleeves with cuffs, gathered or ungathered, others embroidered or plain, handkerchiefs by the dozen, not to mention the purses and gold and silver belts, richly worked, pins, a mirror, a powder box, a comb, a sponge and mucilage for laying hair, an ivory bodkin, a pair of silver tweezers for plucking out little hairs when they appear, a magnifying mirrror for making up her face, and a rag for cleaning it with spittle. (113–14)

Both the preachers and Martínez see, in Professor Owst's words, that "the centre of evil attraction is woman."[60] Both mercilessly accuse her of disobedience, impertinence, garrulity, lust, avarice, drunkenness, envy, slander, and, of course, sinful vanity.[61] The *Whip* and the late medieval popular sermon, then, have in common the denunciation and exemplification of woman's alleged destructiveness. Moreover, rather than a simple, straightforward condemnation, there seems to be a psychological ambivalence at the heart of Martínez's and the preachers' disparagement. Lesley Byrd Simpson remarks that our author approaches the feminine problem like "the reformed rake reliving his rakish past with many a nostalgic glance over his shoulder, beating his breast and sighing the while."[62] Martínez is indeed attracted and repelled. Not surprisingly, this is usually the tone conveyed by the popular preachers. Woman is often the insistent focal point of the sermon—the spellbinding, fascinating object of concern to the celibate homilists. She is the tempting forbidden fruit. She is the Virgin Mary; yet she is also, in the words of the *Laymen's Mirror*, "the behemouth who steals man's soul."[63]

Martínez's delight in picturing the feminine character owes a great debt to the medieval art of preaching. In an oration cited by Owst, for example, a preacher intrigued by the subject of women even takes morbid pleasure, like our author, in graphically describing a disgusting, lust-crazed old crone: "her breth foule stynkyne and her eyen blered, scabbed and febyll, as old wommen buthe."[64] This repulsive portrait immediately brings to mind a strikingly similar one in the *Whip* where an old hag is described in equally vivid terms as a "lecherous bag of bones . . . with her wrinkled belly, her stinking mouth and rotten teeth!" (191). The pulpit and the *Whip* are fascinated by all manner and forms of womankind, and both hold a gross and materialistic view of it. In his famous reprimands, accusations, and incessantly detailed portrayal of the vices, blemishes, and perverse character of bad women, Martínez bears a pronounced resemblance to the satirical, yet altogether seduced, preachers who heaped verbal abuse upon them during the last centuries of the Middle Ages. The *Whip* and the sermon tradition both regard woman as the reprehensible, but nevertheless irresistible, source of all evil.[65]

The fact that the Archpriest's ironic enumeration of feminine cosmetics finds its immediate textual source in the *Fates of Illustrious Men,* and that many of the points of departure for his imprecations against women are found in the "Rejection of Love," are not sufficient grounds, we believe, for wholly explaining his manner and exuberance in maligning women. Although at times textually based on cultivated precedents, his diatribes and exempla received equal inspiration and reinforcement from the material of the popular pulpit. Indeed, only the conjugation of the erudite, literary antifeminist tradition (Boccaccio, Capellanus, etc.) and the caustic misogynistic satire of the preachers can fully explain Martínez's antifeminist attitudes and illustrative tales.

IV *Fire and Brimstone*

Whereas it is well established that an exacerbated millenarian atmosphere existed throughout all levels of society during the late Middle Ages, no one group contributed more to the proliferation of this idea than the popular preachers. The mournful cries of "these are evil times" (*dies mali sunt*) and "remember death" (*memento mori*) echoed incessantly from the pulpits of Europe.[66] A recurrent theme in the sermons of Vincent Ferrer, a notable prophet of doom, was "the end of the world is coming soon, very soon" (Chabás, IX, 99). Eventually, these and similar sentiments found their way into literature and are reflected in the *Archpriest of Talavera*. From the outset, a strong thematic note in Martínez's work is a pessimistic, indeed apocalyptic, vision of the world. In his prologue, for example, he sadly observes that "the end of the world is at hand. Privileges, laws, friendship, kinship, and neighborliness are no longer a deterrent for [the sin of lust], and everything is headed straight for the burning" (14). Like the preachers, our author insistently invokes the Last Days in his pleas for repentance and reform (see, in addition, Part IV, Chapter 1, GM, 230, 234). His millenarian foreboding is undoubtedly rooted in the sermon tradition.

The pervading message of fire and brimstone in the medieval preacher's homilies led him to prefer themes of terror and denunciation, all the while picturing the truly alarming moral decay of the times in his exempla. In a sense, he became the public conscience of Europe during the turbulent fourteenth and fifteenth centuries. The pulpit was a forum for rebuking all of society's evils, and satire was its main weapon. Some of the fiercest satires of the corrupt medieval Church, for instance, are found not in secular literature but in sermons. And it was doubtless this same critical spirit that inspired the anticlerical barbs in the *Whip*. Martínez's parade of "fat priests . . . rich and well dressed" (143), and his cardinals who wait for the pope's death "like famished wolves in February" (GM, 256) reveal a humorous, albeit (to the modern reader) grotesque, anticlericalism that closely resembles that of the popular sermon. In a discourse cited by Lecoy de la Marche, for example, Geoffroi of Troyes even pictures a decadent clergyman with imagery very similar to that used by Martínez: "Immersed in the affairs of the world, he is not preoccupied by those of the spirit. . . . His tonsure, his clothes, his language, all give him a superficial aspect of religion. His true mark is that of the hypocrite, the ravenous wolf."[67] Moreover, in a great many medieval sermons, clerics, like those exemplified in the *Whip*, are accused of simony, gluttony, thievery, fornication, and a host of additional misdemeanors.[68]

Martínez's attacks on clerical immorality are usually light-handed, oblique in comparison to the zealous diatribes of some preachers, although he still manages to satirically portray the lecherous irresponsibility of the churchman who brazenly lies with his "mistress until high noon," and eats and drinks with her in bed when he has "been called to say early Mass, or matins, or vespers" (85). Anticlericalism and anticlerical exempla are motifs that repeat themselves throughout the *Whip*, for our author, like the preachers, saw fit to denounce the frequent lust, hypocrisy, and abuses of the decaying clergy.

Apart from criticizing immoral churchmen, the Archpriest also paints satirical portraits of the people and customs of everyday life that in theme and tone are closely akin to those found in sermons. Because of this portrayal of the commonplace, Menéndez y Pelayo feels that our author was an immediate precursor of the picaresque.[69] This opinion accords with Miguel Herrero García's hypothesis that the picaresque novel is a descendant of the homiletic tradition. The latter notes that "the moral exposition in sermons alternates with descriptions of sinners, anecdotes, exempla, and admonitions, the horrifying or burlesque depiction of the vices, real or imagined naturalistic observations of the human comedy, with which the preacher gives life and plasticity to his lesson. In the picaresque novels the identical elements reciprocate, and the function of the fictional dimension is one and the same as that of exempla in sermons."[70] Although lacking a plot and consistently developed characters, the *Whip*, with its moralizing and exemplification, as well as its quasi-autobiographical point of view, does indeed represent an important bridge between preaching and works like the *Lazarillo de Tormes* and the *Guzmán de Alfarache*, especially the latter. Martínez's sermonic tales herald the satirical vision of humanity conveyed by the picaresque novel's undermining of the quotidian, and that genre's fondness for moralization.

The Archpriest ridicules vices, follies, and stupidities in commonplace social types through shrewd observation. As in the popular sermon and the later picaresque, no one in the community is exempt from the fury of his attacks. Martínez undermines morally reprehensible conduct in all walks of life with graphically sketched, critical caricatures deriving from the preaching tradition. His most acrimonious invective is directed at Beghards and Beguines, familiar sects of laymen often considered the roots of Protestantism[71] and often attacked in sermons. In his exempla they appear as Janus-faced, perverted religious zealots, and in their pious actions they recall the Blindman's mockery of prayer in the *Lazarillo de Tormes* (Chapter 1):

> But, alas, they dissimulate their evil and feign goodness with their habits, their soft words and measured gestures, their eyes downcast as if in an expression of piety, when in reality they are glancing to the side. Devout, prayerful, arbiters of peace, implementors of pious works, religious hangers-on, alter-gnawers, on their hands and knees with their eyes directed toward heaven, fiercely beating their breasts, crying, whimpering, and sighing all the while. Many of these Beghards are of two types: some give themselves to playing the role of the man with other men, desiring men in order to perform their vile deed. Others are like flirtacious little women in their manner and disordered appetities, wanting a man with greater ardor than a woman of ill repute. (GM, 233)[72]

But our preacher's censures are often less severe, turning to humorous satire, as when he portrays the folly of the courtly lover. In this exemplum the acute powers of psychological observation found in sermons shines through, for nothing is ever too trivial for the homilist's ironical descriptions:

Tell me now, and God save you, have you ever seen a lover who was not haughty, proud, and boastful, so much so that no one must bespeak him without permission, holding all others in scorn, as if they were nothing and the sons of no one, save him alone? His speech high-sounding and pompous, accompanied with grimaces and gestures, and he rising on his toes and stretching out his neck, lifting his eyebrows with eloquence and arrogance, scowling when he hears or sees something not to his taste, very ready in threats to kill and cut throats, so that none dares stand before him? And when he mounts his horse (if his rank be such) and rides through the streets, sparing neither donkey nor ass, or the poor and ill-clad, but bumping them all most rudely without pity or compassion, with the pride and fancy that he has from his lady's love? Very erect in the saddle, his legs stuck out, his feet withdrawn from the stirrups, and he glancing down at them ever and anon, if by chance he is wearing his high boots, and these well greased, his hand on his hip, on his head a great Italian biretta, or a hat like a crown, taking up the whole street with his trotting nag, hack, or mule, striking with his spurs, legs, or feet all those he meets and knocking them about and shouting: "Out of the way, there! Long live my lovely mistress!" (78–79)

Like the sharp-tongued, merciless preachers, Martínez reviews the gamut of society. With a few deft touches he evokes the customs and people that surround him. Their idiosyncrasies, faults, indiscretions, and sometimes sinister characteristics are chronicled in vivid detail. His love of depicting the commonplace and ordinary doubtless came to him from his familiarity with the art of preaching. As Keith Whinnom notes, "the exploitation of daily experience . . . through the medium of comparisons and exempla based on quotidian life is typical of vernacular preaching in the last centuries of the Middle Ages."[73]

V *Pulpit Realism*

The medieval pulpit's insistence on using graphic satire and invective as a moral remedy leads G. R. Owst to conclude that it is an important source of literary realism. It is, he says, "in the sphere of satiric representation that... we find common ground between Realism of preacher and artist."[74] And indeed, seen in this light it is clear why the *Whip* has so often been considered an important antecedent of the realist narrative. Like the sermons of the preachers, the work makes continuous use of such realistic devices as direct colloquial speech and detailed plastic descriptions of mundane, familiar people, actions, and situations in order to give life and immediacy to the abstract tenets of Christian morality. Throughout, there is a love of even exaggerated graphic detail that occasionally tends more to grotesque caricature than true realism. Nevertheless, Martínez's propensity to overstate particulars coincides with yet a similar attitude found in the sermon tradition, for as Lecoy de la Marche states, "he who attempts to correct should demand more than what is expected in return; thus, rather than attenuate defects, [the preacher] places them under a magnifying glass."[75]

Betraying his spiritual and artistic kinship to the pulpit, the Archpriest magnifies vice and corruption while supplying a superabundance of the repulsive images, sounds, and smells that accompany them. A passing reference to drunken women, for example, evokes a naturalistic image worthy of the intensely realistic popular sermons: "She who drinks immoderately has a stinking breath, her hands tremble, her senses are dulled, she sleeps little and eats less, and her whole life is given up to drinking and endless scolding" (152). A decrepit old man married to a comely young girl is described with the utmost care as a "hawking and spitting old fool, heavy as lead, full of depravities... putrid old goat, accursed of God and His saints, bent and sluggish, dirty... rough as shark skin, stiff as an ox, potbellied as a gander, gray, bald, and toothless... a cold pig, sweating in summer and shivering in winter" (192–93). In another exemplum, Martínez reveals the shocking particulars of how a case of infanticide was discovered. The child was killed by the mother's lover, "and he and the mother buried him in a stable. A pig dug the body up later..." (68). Martínez's intensely realistic treatment of sordid detail, derived from sermonic tradition, never spares his reader the minute accounting of a wretched story.

The Archpriest, however, does not always limit himself to grotesqueries. Less unpleasant, although equally intense, satiric and ironic details inundate his exempla. Indeed, it is the passing idiosyncrasy, the often unnoticed particular, that is the prime mover in delineating the realistic characters who populate the *Whip.* We have already seen the courtly lover with his Italian biretta and well-greased boots, a case where clothes really do make the man. When closely scrutinized, the seemingly unimportant objects of his attire are not functionless superficialities. Rather, they are the very key to character, the objective correlatives of a definite attitude and life-style. In all his exempla, Martínez keenly recognizes the possibilities of graphic description as a function of characterization. An ostensibly insignificant, vulgar action, for instance, may contrast with the words a character speaks, and hence betray his inner thoughts. A clear example of this appears in an anecdote recounting how a woman coerces her lover into a duel with someone she feels has insulted her. Martínez tells us that in such situations "the lover [often] kills or gets killed, he cuts or gets cut, and the whole business is nothing but trouble for both sides. And when he is brought back to her house wounded or having wounded, the blessed promoter of it all scratches her arse (speaking with due reverence) and says: 'Unhappy creature that I am, shamed and undone'" (183). The vivacity, directness, and detail of Martínez's word-pictures thus hold the reader's attention, for they reveal, like those of the popular preachers, a direct contact with life—the mainstay of literary realism.[76]

As opposed to the stylized images and characters in the works of his Spanish contemporaries, the Archpriest's masterpiece projects an earthy familiarity akin to that of the popular sermon. The *Whip*'s realistic, innovative handling of the commonplace in picturesque, forceful language owes much to the medieval homiletic tradition, for the preachers were also uncanny observers and artful chroniclers of the incidental but revealing detail. Moreover, the high-spirited, graphic anecdotes, the genuinely antiheroic portraits, the living voices of the people in the *Archpriest of Talavera* all surge forth from the same intent as that of the sermon: the desire to instruct while entertaining—didacticism at its best.[77]

In summation, the *Whip* reflects the most profound and enduring stylistic, thematic, and structural influence of the pulpit. It is a work, as we have seen, that closely follows the example of preaching as set forth in the *artes praedicandi* (arts of preaching) and popular sermons of the late Middle Ages. Martínez's familiarity with homiletic themes and techniques is not surprising, especially if his canonical university education, clerical status, and self-confessed visits to the Crown of Aragon are taken into account. This kingdom was a great center of sermonic activity during the fourteenth and fifteenth centuries, and the home of three of the most distinguished preachers of the medieval pulpit: Ramón Llull, Vincent Ferrer, and Françesc Eiximenis. Even if the Archpriest did not study the arts of preaching firsthand (a doubtful conjecture), he would simply have had to listen to sermons in order to grasp their style, structural principles, themes, and formulae. Whatever the case may be, given his great interest in religious polemics associated with the Dominicans and Franciscans, the two great medieval preaching orders,[78] it is not unreasonable to assume that Martínez de Toledo was impressed by the didactic, as well as artistic, potentials of pulpit oratory, and utilized its methods in writing the *Archpriest of Talavera.*

CHAPTER 5

Courtly Love and Orthodoxy in the Whip

FROM the very beginning of the *Whip* it is clear that Martínez has one aim in mind—the reprobation of worldly love. Yet the satirical portraits he paints throughout the work frequently ridicule the refined and formalized amatory manners practiced by European aristocracy during the waning of the Middle Ages. By worldly love, then, we believe Martínez was referring not only to lust in general but also to the idealized medieval conception of love known in academic circles today as courtly love.

I *The Ritualization of Love*

The term "courtly love" is a familiar one to students of medieval literature. Definitions of it have been attempted by numerous scholars, although there seems to be considerable disagreement among them as to the precise characteristics of the concept.[1] Indeed, one critic, E. Talbot Donaldson, has challenged its existence altogether; another, Peter Dronke, has recently emphasized its pervasiveness and universality.[2] The latter denies that it was an aristocratic medieval attitude originating in twelfth-century Provence as previously believed, affirming that the courtly and popular traditions of love are practically inseparable and "possible in any time or place and on any level of society."[3] Yet, while Dronke's arguments and examples are quite convincing, it cannot be denied that a formalized view of love placing woman at its center became fashionable among the nobility of the last centuries of the Middle Ages, and that it was probably popularized by the widespread acceptance of the Provençal lyric. Although the troubadours certainly did not invent the idealization of woman, they did, however, refine and institutionalize it, making it part and parcel of medieval palace manners and morals.

The medieval gentility's conception of romantic love fostered by the Provençal literary vogue focuses on man's worship of woman. She is viewed as an overlord, indeed sometimes a divinity, to be respected and revered. "The novelty of Courtly Love," notes A. J. Denomy, "lies in three basic elements: first, in the ennobling force of human love; second, in the elevation of the beloved to a place of superiority above the lover; third, in the conception of love as ever unsatiated, ever increasing desire."[4] Like a code of ethics, its observance purifies, ennobles the lover and casts virtue upon him. As in any ethical system promising reward, certain qualities and conditions must be met in order for the lover to be worthy of the beloved. He should be faithful, courageous, discreet, humble, youthful, courteous, handsome, generous, and eloquent.

The fifteenth-century Castilian poets Fernando de la Torre, Hernando de Ludueña, and Suero de Ribera sum up the requirements in a composite picture of the ideal lover. De la Torre notes that he should be "a discreet and polished young man / brave, dextrous and daring, / virtuous and moderate, / well liked by other men, / but well loved by the ladies, / praised by them / in public and in private" (*Discreto galán polido, / valiente, diestro y osado, / virtuoso, bien medido, / de los onbres muy querido, / de las damas más amado, / por todas mucho loado / en público e escondido*).[5] Hernando de Ludueña gives special consideration to the lover's youth: "The suitor should be / first of such an age / that he is not older than thirty-six / not so young that he / might destroy wisdom with frivolity, / because he was not yet humbled by experience. / If he has a gallant / disposition it is certain he will triumph; / he will lack all if wanting of discretion" (*El galán ha de tener / lo primero tal hedad / que de treynta y seys no passe; / no tan moço que el saber / destruya con liuiandad, / porque no se despompasse. / Si con gentil condición / tuuiere disposición, / es cierto que ganará; / mas todo le falta / si le falta discreción*).[6] Ribera emphasizes elegance and eloquence in lovers in the form of musical and poetic accomplishments: "They should be very discreet, / well shod, well dressed, / witty and intrepid, / prudent, frank, and secretive; / very chaste and courteous, / capable of elegant inventions, / good couplets and songs, / discreet in all their trappings" (*Deuen ser mucho discretos, / bien calçados, bien vestidos, / donosos e ardidos, / cuerdos, francos e secretos; / muy onestos e corteses, / de gentiles inuenciones, / buenas coplas e canciones, / discretos mucho en arneses*).[7] Similarly, the woman must be "perfect in all her attributes. . . . Her hair is blond or golden; her eyes beautiful; her complexion fresh and clear; her mouth rosy and smiling; her flesh white, soft, and smooth; her body slender, well formed, and without blemish. . . . In short all that makes a perfect woman."[8] It is a love based primarily on physical beauty, "a conception of pure love of desire arising from the contemplation of the beauty of the beloved and effecting the union of the minds and hearts of the lovers."[9]

The medieval aristocratic lover is generally expected to perform noble deeds in the name of his lady, but he sometimes suffers because she often remains indifferent or, even if she favors his adoration, because respect for her prevents consummation of their love. Ideally, he should keep secret the beloved's name, although he carries her scarf or some other favor or celebrates her beauty in poetry. This is because she is usually married to someone else. A common aspect of the code seems to be the incompatibility of love with marriage.[10] A refined, aristocratic conception of romantic passion, it essentially postulates the worship of a courtier for a beautiful, lofty-minded noblewoman.

This formalized vision of love, then, accords the lady the respect commanded by an overlord to whom homage should be paid. The relationship is often carried one step further, however, in that she is sometimes granted the status of a god. "In essence," June Hall Martin observes, courtly love "is a christianization of a pagan religion. The courtly lady is adored as the Christian adores God. The lover is constantly seeking her grace, or her 'mercy'; at times he even prostrates himself before her in an attitude of worship. . . . On one level she assumes the role of lord in the feudal sense; on a higher level she becomes Lord in the religious sense."[11]

Andreas Capellanus's *Art of Courtly Love* is traditionally recognized as the first attempt to define that set of chivalrous erotic conventions known to us as courtly love. It was a work that had vast appeal during the later Middle Ages, and one that was not unknown to fifteenth-century Castilian authors other than Martínez de Toledo. Expressing the opinion that honor can only come from virtue, for example, Juan Rodríguez del Padrón cites Andreas's "first book" as testimony of a well-known authority in support of his argument.[12] Moreover, Otis H. Green has irrefutably confirmed the existence of courtly amatory attitudes in mid-fifteenth-century Castilian poetry that are very similar to those outlined by Capellanus. Indeed, he has demonstrated how they were not only present, but in fact endemic to the romantic beliefs of the poets at the literary court of Juan II.[13]

This type of formalized romantic passion was not merely a literary posture totally divorced from Castilian reality but, rather, very much a part of palace manners and values at Juan's court. The observance of courtly ritual, especially the service of love, became particularly fashionable during Juan's reign, although it had long been considered a source of virtue by the Spanish nobility. Alfonso the Learned's thirteenth-century codification of Castilian law, *Las siete partidas* (*Seven Divisions*), for instance, notes that "in order to increase their courage in battle, knights should remember the ladies whom they served so that their spirits might be fortified and they might have greater fear of unworthy deeds."[14] Moreover, the mid-fourteenth-century epic *Poema de Alfonso XI* (*Poem of Alfonso XI*) extols the ennobling power of an idealized, extramarital love;[15] and, as we have mentioned, the *Book of Good Love* contains many elements of the romantic love tradition.

But it is during the fifteenth century that courtly values seem to have reached their maximum degree of acceptance and expression in Castile. A clear indication of this can be found, not only in the poetry written at Juan II's court, but in a remarkable historical work composed just four years prior to the *Whip*, Pero Rodríguez de Lena's *Libro del passo honroso* (*Book of the Honorable Passage*). This work reveals just how fashionable idealized love had become, for it recounts how a young knight named Suero de Quiñones was granted permission by King Juan to defend a bridge against all comers in homage to the lady he loved. Sixty-eight knights challenged him during the month-long siege, and many were wounded and one killed. Although the incident sounds very much like a fantastic medieval romance, it did in fact occur. And what is more significant, it seems to have stirred no reaction from his contemporaries: evidently Quiñones's conduct was considered a matter of course.[16] The romantic apotheosis of woman and the concomitant service owed her (courtly love) was indeed far more than a literary game played by the Castilian nobility. To all appearances, it was a social reality, an accepted form of normal behavior, and not an abstract, aesthetic dilettantism.

II *Idealized Love and Heterodoxy*

The acknowledgment and formalization of the amatory conventions we have outlined above led to the creation of what might be called a cult of love—a cult in many ways paralleling and even sacrilegiously adopting Christian principles and rituals in the worship of the beloved. An erotic religion arose as a rival or parody of Christianity.[17] At the time Martínez de Toledo was writing his reprobation, other authors were composing devotionary works in celebration of romantic love. In a curious syncretism of liturgical, theological, and amatory concepts, Castilian poets wrote *Ten Commandments of Love,*[18] *Masses of Love,*[19] *Sermons of Love,*[20] eroticized *Lesson on the Book of Job,*[21] and *Miserere*'s to the god of love,[22] along with countless other profane adaptations of Christian motifs. There even existed Orders of Love (similar in principle to the monastic orders), pilgrimages to the shrine of martyred lovers, and general councils of love.[23] Indeed, romantic love was so closely identified with Christianity that a poet's mistress could be equated with salvation, or even implied to be like Christ Himself.[24] Juan II's confidant, Alvaro de Luna, was known to have placed his beloved in a position superior to God's, remarking that if God should ever seek a mistress He would be his competitor for the favors of his lady. Moreover, the apotheosis of woman as the personification of the highest form of moral good was not limited in practice to secular authors. Clerics like Fray Diego de Valencia and the Cardinal of Valencia wrote amorous paens honoring the married ladies whom they served.[25] The conception of love articulated and defended by these contemporaries of Martínez de Toledo was, of course, anathema to Christian morality and ritual.

Kenelm Foster observes that "it is clear that in so far as courtly love was an attempt to vindicate for the sexual impulse an intrinsic value, a potential moral worth apart from its procreative purpose, it could look for no support from contemporary theology."[26] With this and the literary profanations of Christian devotion we have cited in mind, we can see how it would have been indeed strange had the Church not raised its voice in protest: and in fact it did, in the person of Alfonso Martínez de Toledo. As chaplain to King Juan, he served in an atmosphere charged with courtly eroticism and almost decadent literary refinement.[27] He was doubtless alarmed by the doctrinal implications of the love practiced around him, and wrote the *Archpriest of Talavera* in order to combat what he thought was the encroaching heterodoxy of idealized passion. The worldly love he attacks in his treatise is often the fashionable code of amatory ethics held by his peers—the exalted, romantic eroticism of medieval gentility which was very much a reality and which students of the Middle Ages today call courtly love.

The cultivation of a refined amatory literature was in great part responsible for the proliferation of courtly love ideals at Juan II's court and Martínez de Toledo is the first to recognize it. He is quick to point out how his work is "not a chronicle or romance of chivalry, in which at times white is made black" (96)—that is to say, in which lust is shown to be something other than what it is by concealing it under hieratic manners. What he seeks to demonstrate is the truth behind the gallant illusion, the degradation and sin hidden in the rhetorical idealization of love and woman. Although Christine J. Whitbourn falls short of concluding that the *Whip* might have arisen out of the need to counter the existence of what moralists considered a devotion of love rivaling the Church and flourishing in the urbane atmosphere of King Juan's court, she analyzes Martínez's parody of the idealized literary love tradition. She observes that "the lover whom [Martínez] constantly ridicules has many of the conventional characteristics of the idealized lover" and that "he refers also to the idea of servitude which was essential to the tradition," while "the courtly requisites of singing and versifying are also mentioned."[28] She notes that Martínez's phlegmatic man represents a direct contradiction of the typical courtly lover. Although professing noble pretensions, he is neither courageous, discreet, refined, nor generous.[29] In fact, the Archpriest's lovers are all self-centered, defamatory, indiscreet, violent, pusillanimous, and the epitome of sensuality. If you propose anything that does not lead to the lover's immediate gratification, Martínez tells us,

> at such a moment the anger of a lover is so great that it cannot be contained, especially if his mistress has not responded to his advances, or he becomes so morose that if he can get some unlucky man or woman into a dispute, he will most likely bury them under the sod. . . . Others, from anger and melancholy, slash at the dogs and animals they happen to pass. Still others shatter their swords on the stones from pure rage, and bite their cheeks and lips, grind their teeth, and shoot fire from their eyes. Or they beat and abuse their mules and horses; or they neglect to feed them until night; or they strike them over the head with the peck measure—all this from rage and ill temper, because their mistress did not yield to them or looked crossly at them, and they say: "Damn the whore and daughter of a whore! She gave me the eye, she winked at me, she did this and that, and now she throws me over! She says 'Come here' with her eyes and holds me off with her hands. By God's body, the devil must have got me into this mess!" (84)

Martínez's lovers all possess an inflated concept of their own nobility, yet in action they prove their ignominy and lack of responsibility for the honor of the beloved. Rather than pay homage to her, for instance, the songs they compose bring public disrepute to the beloved as well as the lover: "They disgrace themselves with their noisiness, their playing and singing in the streets and squares, and shouting for all the world to hear: 'Look at me! I'm in love with What's-her-name and I want you to know it!' As if they were reading a royal edict" (86). The unquestioned fidelity owed the lady is also mocked, for the lover with noble airs is, like the sanguine man, in reality capricious, inconstant, and blasphemous: "Since he is gay and pleasure-loving, he is very lecherous and his heart burns like fire, and he loves to the left and to the right. Every woman he sees he loves and desires, and with all of them he is very gay, justifying himself by what the prophet David says in his Psalm: '*For Thou, O Lord, hast made me glad through Thy work.* Therefore, O Lord, if I love, I love and desire the woman who is beautiful, for she is the work of Thy hands, and, since the prophet so commands, O Lord, I should not be sinning' " (176). The satisfaction of an unrestrained appetite "is the reason for all their parties, balls, and dances, all their merrymaking, their singing and playing, all their love letters and joustings and tourneys and bullfights, their feasts, their fine clothes and better boots, and the rest—all of which has the single purpose of winning those they love best, merely to betray them. Moreover, once they have succeeded, how many dishonest acts of lechery they commit, not to be mentioned here or described" (72–73). Throughout the *Whip* the image of the courtly lover is systematically undermined. He is exemplified as an ignoble, greedy, rationalizing, and even ridiculous creature motivated by the basest aspirations.

In their ethopoeias of the ideal lover, de la Torre, Ribera, and Ludueña emphasize, as we have seen, eloquence, good physical proportions, youth, elegance, discretion and honesty. Describing the various appearances of men, Martínez paints his composite picture of them in a different light:

> Curly-haired or red-haired or prematurely gray; round or long-headed; brows wrinkled or with cowlicks or hair growing very low on them; eye-brows meeting; flat noses, *canusos*, or great long noses, or thin and sharp noses; deep-set eyes, small with scanty lashes, or red, or spotted; large mouth; lisping or stuttering speech; teeth sharp and uneven; cleft chin; face wide and round; large dangling ears; heavy protruding jaw; prematurely bearded; neck short and thick; one-eyed or cross-eyed or squinting in both eyes; lame or stoop-shouldered or hump-backed, single or double; the body covered with hair, or hairless and smooth; wide hips; crooked legs; malformed hands and feet; soft- or hasty-spoken; demeanor calm or excitable; lying; haughty, and so many other characteristics that it would take a great while to tell you what each one signifies. (174)

The characteristics men possess for Martínez preclude all those expected of the courtly lover. In fact, his archetypal man bears all the anomalies of a wild man similar to those personifying lust in late Gothic iconography.

It is woman, however, the bestower of bogus virtue and the false idol revered by courtly lovers, that clearly holds the most interest and bears the full force of Martínez's attack. The Archpriest's unequivocal accusations of her diabolical nature are intended to strike at the heart of courtly ideals. They are designed to contradict that idealized picture of femininity held by the partisans of the romantic conception of love. Passion's inspiration in a woman's beauty, a fundamental tenet of courtly beliefs, is assailed by exemplifying how her physical perfection is in essence false. The result is the long passage on cosmetics adapted from Boccaccio.[30] Moreover, rather than being the lofty-minded, discriminating embodiment of virtue, beautiful women "take up with base, ugly, poor, luckless, and worthless men, crippled, one-armed or one-eyed, and even hunchbacks" (55). Woman is deceitful and hypocritical, the reverse of the honorable paragon of the courtly tradition since "it is not to be doubted that [she] has two faces, or is a double-edged knife, for we see every day that she says one thing with her mouth, but has something different in her heart" (128). Her motive in love is not the quest of moral perfection posited by the romantics, but "to get and possess, because that is her nature, for most women are avaricious and when they get their hands on something they never let it go. They love temporal riches to a superlative degree, and to get money and keep it they put their minds and bodies to some very cunning uses, and in this they are most diligent and clever" (57). Humility and charity are certainly not to be found in her because "so great is her pride that she has no respect for any woman whatever; rather she scorns them all and esteems them not at all. One she calls low; another filthy; another of no account; another lazy; another slovenly; another wicked; another backbiter, and she herself is perhaps worse than any of them. She finds faults in others, but not in herself" (139). Her femininity is her best excuse for license: "They protect themselves by saying: 'I am a woman; he won't molest me; he won't strike me or draw his sword against me, for I am a woman and he would be dishonored if he did such a thing, because a man should not attack or use force on a woman, Jew, or priest, for they are weak and helpless creatures.' And this is why a woman will frequently dare to dishonor, vilify, or defame a man" (138). The iconoclastic picture of woman painted by Martínez is that of a petty, stubborn, treacherous, egotistical, bothersome, lustful being. She is the exact moral antithesis of the courtly ideal.

The denunciation of love and women was carried to its extreme by moralists and theologians during the zenith of courtly love.[31] While medieval romantics were defining love as a form of desire of the beloved (see *Art of Courtly Love*, Book I, Chapter 1), theologians equated desire with sin and concupiscence.[32] They doubtless saw in the exaltation of the moral superiority and desirability of woman an alarming form of heterodoxy. Christianity had always assigned woman a secondary, supportive role to man. She was a helpmate; her place was in marriage and the home. The courtly conception of love reversed this image of her and pictured her as an overlord and source of virtue. This was enough to bring idealized love into conflict with the Church and touch off a reaction aimed at reasserting her traditional role.

It is not surprising therefore that the *Whip* bears distinctly antifeminist leanings. Other than the advocacy of the love of God, one of Martínez's primary intentions in writing it was to demonstrate how the romantics' idol of adoration (woman) did indeed have clay feet. Despite protestations to the contrary, it is a notably misogynistic work, and this is principally because the Archpriest likely conceived his attack on courtly beliefs in terms of their priorities. He concentrates on woman since his first desire was to demythologize the demiurge of the cult of love. It is not until this is thoroughly accomplished that the worshiper (man) is reproached for his truancy. Even then, his exempla reproving men usually turn out to be markedly antifeminist. His male portraits are not so complex or exuberant as those of women. This, however, is probably not because he lacked literary precedents, as Miss Whitbourn contends,[33] but because men are clearly of less ethical importance in the error of courtly love. The suppliant is clearly less culpable than the graven image.

Throughout his work, the Archpriest "reveals a preoccupation with the tradition of idealized love, but it is the preoccupation of one determined to discredit it."[34] His aim is the exemplification of the fact that beneath the idolization of woman and the urbanity of the fashionable love ritual lies a smoldering passion. He tells his readers that despite the gallantries, songs, refined manners, and declarations of noble intentions, the prime mover of romantic love is lust. An orthodox Christian and a skeptic to boot, Martínez felt that the polished words, gestures, and civility of his contemporaries masked unequivocally erotic sentiments. As a cleric responsible for the moral ambient at King Juan's court, he therefore marshaled all the resources, expressive powers, and erudition at his disposal to challenge the idealized beliefs and create an *ars amatoria* ("art of loving") in consonance with medieval Christian ethics.

His satirical refutation of lust concentrates vigorously on romantic love's sinfulness and affirms the superiority of divine love. He specifically alludes to the wickedness of believing in woman's divinity and the lover's adoration of her. Love, he tells us, is "the cause of worshipping strange gods and of idolatry" (34–35). Later, he again concludes "that he who loves another more than God scorns his creator and places the creature above Him; he casts virtue aside and loves sin, and, moreover, trespasses against His First Commandment" (63). It is clear that Martínez is conscious of the heterodox implications of the amatory philosophy flourishing around him. For him, courtly love is not a principle of moral development, but its converse. It precludes the attainment of the seven virtues and compliance with the Decalogue, while it leads to the commission of the seven deadly sins and undermines the powers of the soul. Its consequences are all doctrinal and all transcendent—it strikes at the very marrow of Christianity.

The Archpriest takes particular pains to argue against one of the most heterodox theses expounded by the defenders of idealized love—its fatefulness. The romantic love practiced by his contemporaries was believed by some to be caused by Providence. Otis Green demonstrates how the poets of the fifteenth century often proclaimed love's inevitability, imputing its presence to the influence of Fortune and the workings of the stars.[35] Our author, hence, goes out of his way to establish the superiority of reason and especially volition over nature, affirming the existence of freedom of choice in Part IV of his work. Man is free to reject worldly love, just as he is free to eschew all manner of sin. And it is in this light that the fourth part of the *Whip* must be viewed. It is not simply a superfluous, "insufferably dull treatise on astrology" written in a "logic-chopping Schoolman's style" as Lesley Byrd Simpson believes,[36] but a fundamental element of Martínez's rebuttal to the un-Christian beliefs held by the partisans of the romantic philosophy of love.[37]

The *Whip* is first and foremost a call for orthodoxy in matters of love inspired by the apostasy of courtly love. As a strictly Christian work, it reaffirms man's freedom of choice and notes that all forms of worldly love are "madness and vanity, for only the love of God gives life, health, wealth, estate, honor, and final glory to him who serves Him and cares not for vanity and madness" (195). Yet, it also, albeit reluctantly, concedes that the sexual appetite is inherent in man, although it should be governed by reason at all times and sanctioned by the sacrament of matrimony. Martínez consistently advises marriage,[38] underlining in his exempla that woman should remain in her place as defined by patristic authority, the Bible, and popular tradition. The alternatives to worldly love he offers in his work are those particularly inimical to the courtly ideal—celibacy or matrimony—and his affirmation of them can be seen as a repudiation of the romantic tradition.

III *The Recovered Palinode*

In our mind, Martínez's use of the "Rejection of Love" (Book III of the *Art of Courtly Love*) as the backbone of his work confirms his desire to specifically reprove courtly love conventions. It was not by chance he chose to gloss and incorporate it into the *Whip*. We have mentioned how Andreas's treatise codifies the precepts of the romantic love tradition in Books I and II, how it was known to the Archpriest's contemporaries, and how it was cited as an authoritative work by one of the great Castilian defenders of love and the superiority of women—Juan Rodríguez del Padrón.

The sole surviving Hispanic manuscript of the *Art of Courtly Love*, the *Regles de amor* (*Rules of Love*), a Catalan translation (ca. 1387) attributed to Domenec Mascó, contains all but the final palinode.[39] It is possible, therefore, that a widespread manuscript tradition reflecting the omission of Book III existed in the Iberian Peninsula during the fourteenth and fifteenth centuries. By its very survival, the Catalan manuscript would tend to corroborate the popularity of this shortened version. If this was in fact the case, one of the most widely circulated vernacular examples of the *Art of Courtly Love* was only partially complete. Edited in this manner, it might naturally have been viewed by its readers as a wholesale affirmation of the philosophy of idealized love. They might also have used it as an authority to vouch for their beliefs and cited it, as did Rodríguez del Padrón, in their defense of feminine moral perfection and the ennobling power of love.

Recognizing this, Martínez might logically have chosen to gloss Book III, the "Rejection of Love," in his reprobation of worldly love.[40] In this way, he could set the record straight, as it were, and effectively oppose one of the principal arguments and authorities of the partisans of idealized passion. If Andreas were ironically turned against them, the adherents to the courtly philosophy of love expressed in Books I and II of Capellanus's tract could do little to counter Martínez's own claims of the heterodoxy of their ideas. For this reason, we believe the mysterious Juan de Ausim mentioned in the *Whip*'s prologue is indeed probably a scribal mistake for Andreas Capellanus. Martínez would in all likelihood have relished the irony and wanted to publicize the moral authority upon whom he was basing his Christian refutation of courtly love.

The *Whip*, then, is a work of great importance, not only in understanding courtly attitudes in Spain and moralists' reactions to them, but in indirectly explaining the probable role Capellanus's treatise played in the formulation of those ideas. Martínez's presumably conscious use of the "Rejection of Love" seems to indicate that Books I and II of the *Art of Courtly*

Love were in fact looked to, if not to define, at least to vouch for the idealization of love and women in fifteenth-century Castile. His work also reveals how some churchmen did indeed feel challenged and alarmed by the fashionable service of love and the defenses they adduced to reaffirm its error. Moreover, it seems to confirm the most recent cynical interpretations of courtly love (notably Whinnom and Foreman), for it offers a contemporary opinion that it was not merely an innocuous literary game but a reality felt by some to be charged with veiled erotic, and even obscene, intentions. In the place of courtly love, it uncompromisingly offers the only forms of love permitted the Christian—either marriage or, preferably, divine adoration in the form of celibacy. Hence the *Whip* is a document not only of literary but of social importance as well. In fact, it is a work of social and religious protest that provides one more insight into the atmosphere of ethical crisis characterizing Spanish society during the waning of the Middle Ages.

CHAPTER 6

The Whip's Literary Legacy

MARTÍNEZ'S orthodox views on love, his good-humored satire, and his literary virtuosity made the *Whip* a work of vital interest to the fifteenth- and sixteenth-century Castilian imagination. While few critical judgments of it survive, there is perhaps no better proof of its popularity than the homage paid to it by contemporary and succeeding literary generations. Like any significant work achieving a degree of acceptance, the *Whip* either directly or indirectly influenced a great many later writers.

I *The Fifteenth Century*

Perhaps the *Whip*'s most significant contribution to the literature of its age lies in its role as the probable stimulus to the great feminist literary controversy of the fifteenth century.[1] In early Castilian letters the theme of woman was, of course, present,[2] but it was not until about 1440 that it became an obsession. From this time on until the end of the century woman was the heated topic of both defenders and detractors. And notably, the sudden proliferation of a feminist literature in Castile occurs immediately following the appearance of the *Archpriest of Talavera* in 1438. Upon reading it, as we noted earlier, Juan II's queen was indignant and appealed for a literary defense of women to counter what she doubtless considered its misogyny. Shortly thereafter, there was a veritable flood of works dedicated to the queen and defending the nobility and superiority of women. In 1443, Juan Rodríguez del Padrón wrote his *Triunfo de las donas* (*Triumph of the Ladies*) in which he outlines fifty often ludicrous reasons for feminine excellence. In his prologue to this work, Juan de Mena tells us it is the direct result of recent slanderous attacks on women, and alludes to Martínez de Toledo as the principal culprit. He accuses him of writing fiction, and of having vituperated women without divine or human reason, and concludes that the Archpriest deserves censure "for having talked too much and written torpid and unchaste fictions."[3] Later, Mosén Diego de Valera alludes to Martínez and "these initiators of a new sect that perversely takes pleasure in generally vituperating women."[4] A record exists of other, now lost, profeminist works probably written as a result of Queen María's outrage at the *Whip*. It is known, for example, that Alonso de Cartagena composed a *Libro de mugeres ilustres* (*Book of Illustrious Women*), and that Andrés, or Antón, Delgadillo defended women in his *Libro de la mugeres* (*Book of Women*).

The most important fifteenth-century vindication of woman, however, has survived to the present day: Alvaro de Luna's *Libro de las virtuosas y claras mujeres* (*Book of Virtuous and Illustrious Women*), ca. 1446. Aside from its didactic pretensions, this work is, like the others we have mentioned, polemical in nature. It is written with the intent of defending woman from her Castilian detractors. Composed in order to "reprehend in immortal script the sinister accusations of those who brazenly doubt and defame women,"[5] it also was probably a direct, if tardy, answer to Queen María's request. In all probability, then, the *Whip* is the central, although not the only, Castilian antifeminist work to have elicited a response from contemporary writers. Since it was "the first extensive misogynistic contribution to Castilian letters,"[6] it doubtless played an important role in provoking the appearance of works in a profeminist vein. If it did not start the fires of the feminist polemic of the 1440s, at the very least it was instrumental in stoking them.

Martínez's part in presumably stimulating the outpouring of works defending women, however, ends with this negative influence. The profeminists inherited little from the *Whip* other than making misogyny their rallying point. On the whole, their compositions are its artistic antithesis—they are abstract, allegorical, narrative, and precious. Luna's work is the prototype of Castilian profeminist literature. Patterned after Boccaccio's *De Claris Mulieribus* (*On Illustrious Women*), it is filled with elegant historical and mythological exempla supported by abstract arguments expounding the virtues of femininity in a highly cultivated language. None of the Archpriest's reasoning, literary devices, and colorful anecdotes influenced the defenders of women, although his tacit marginal presence as the first Castilian maligner of women must have been felt by champions of the sex.

One late profeminist, however, does seem to allude directly to the *Archpriest of Talavera.* In his *Sermón de amor* (*Sermon on Love*), Diego de San Pedro shows an awareness, if not an outright attempt at parody, of the *Whip.* Like the first part of Martínez's treatise, San Pedro's work is a sermon on love; but it is an affirmation of the moral superiority of courtly ideals and women, rather than a reprobation of them. Like Martínez, San Pedro deals with love's effect upon the virtues and its relationship to the Decalogue[7] while unreservedly and almost word for word mocking the *Whip*'s incipit. In direct ironical reference to Martínez's prologue, he begins by noting how "nothing can be well done, well said, begun, half done, or finished" without the grace of love and the "intercession of faith."[8] Martínez, of course, invokes God, the Trinity, and the intercession of the Virgin in almost the exact language.

The Archpriest's literary influence is understandably more direct in the antifeminist camp of the polemic. In his vehemently misogynistic *Repetición de amores* (*Valedictory of Love*), ca. 1485, Luis de Lucena follows a line of argumentation closely akin to the *Whip*'s, although he never mentions our author's work. In an exclamatory style similar to Martínez's, Lucena chides those who love another above God: "Oh, what great evil and what great danger it is to love a being in such a way that we forget God, the only way to heaven! . . . All Christians should eschew illicit love and give themselves to serving only Him."[9] The similarity of the two works, however, does not stop here. On the contrary, a textual analysis of the condemnation of cosmetics in the *Valedictory* reveals that Lucena had the *Whip* in mind when he composed this part of his work. Later, he virtually plagiarizes a description of the coquetries of women from Martínez. Deploring that woman pays little attention to what she does or says, the Archpriest remarks that "at times, as if by accident, she will raise her skirt and show a slipper or a foot or a bit of leg, and then she will look around to see if anyone is watching. And she will pretend that she had only been careless and will drop her skirt and lower her eyes modestly. But she knows well enough what she is doing" (140). Commenting on the studied modesty of women, Lucena observes that "they practice the way they walk . . . and the manner in which, as if by accident, they might show off a foot with a bit of the milky white of their legs; and how they should lower their eyes in timid shame. What gestures they will make! Oh, how they'll laugh!"[10] In short, the *Valedictory* adapts not only the *Whip*'s theme and elements of its style, but even entire passages from it.

Another fifteenth-century antifeminist receiving a considerable influence from Martínez is Rodrigo de Reinosa, a popular balladeer. In his pioneer study on the *Whip*, Erich von Richthofen was the first to notice that a broadside attributed to Reinosa is a poetic reworking of the Archpriest's famed exemplum in which a woman bewails the loss of an egg.[11] Reinosa's *Coplas que hablan de cómo las mugeres por una cosa de no nada dicen muchas cosas, en 'special una muger sobre un huevo con su criada* (*Couplets Which Tell How Women Will Talk Ceaselessly About a Trifle, Especially a Woman to Her Servant About an Egg*) reveal a truly remarkable dependence on our author's text, for they adapt not only the situation but entire phrases recalling the interrogative and exclamatory tone of the original:

> Oh, woe is me and fraught with worry,
> They've stolen my egg
> my egg worth a farthing!
>   On with you, Mariquilla, you whore,
> You're the liar who ate it . . .
> You with your bright red shamed face.
> Why did you ruin me? . . .
> Oh, why don't I kill you?
>   Oh, my polished egg,
> that such a fool would have it.
> How did I ever lose you?
> Pray to God that whosoever ate you
> should himself be eaten! . . .

It was white as crystal
with a heavy shell. . . .
  Oh, what a hen or rooster
might have issued from you, my egg!
Oh, woe is me, poor and sad;
I tell you, friend and neighbor,
it was worth a newly minted ducat!

(*¡ay amarga con cuidado,*
qué huevo me ha hurtado
que valía un maravedí! . . .
  Anda, puta Mariquilla,
que tu falsa lo comiste . . .
carillos rostros de brasa,
¿por qué me echas a perder? . . .
¿cómo no te mato yo? . . .
  ¡Ay mi huevo tan pulido
que en tal bellaca se emplea;
cómo te habré perdido
plega a Dios quien t' ha comido
que mal comido se vea! . . .
blanco era como el cristal
y la cáscara muy gruesa. . . .
  ¡Ay qué gallo y qué gallina
saliera de vos, mi huevo!
¡ay de mí, triste mezquina!
sabed, comadre y vecina,
que valía un real nuevo!)[12]

Indeed, the kinship of the two works is so great that Reinosa even preserves the monologue form and the character of Mariquilla, the young servant girl evoked, though not described, in Martínez's passage. In the final analysis, however, the Archpriets's original version of the episode is far more dramatic than the one we find in the ballad.

A second ballad attributed to Reinosa, the *Coplas de las comadres* (*Couplets of the Go-betweens*), also evinces an influence from the *Whip.*[13] A reproach of cosmetics similar to Martínez's and characters fitting his description of a typical procuress appear in this work. However, this poem adapts the material more liberally from its model than the *Couplets Which*

Tell How a Woman Will Talk Ceaselessly. Although Reinosa's use of dialogue and monologue, his portraits of the women, and his strong antifeminist statements recall the *Whip*, a closer resemblance to passages in *Tragicomedia de Calisto y Melibea* (*Tragicomedy of Calisto and Melibea*), or *Celestina*, is more obvious.[14]

Martínez de Toledo's influence on the *Celestina* and its possible implications have long been neglected. Von Richthofen recently reemphasized the *Archpriest of Talavera*'s fundamental relationship to this work, but his important study seems to have had no appreciable impact on contemporary scholarship.[15] Early critics like Wolf and Menéndez y Pelayo perceived and commented upon the kinship of the two works. Cejador y Frauca, in his edition of Rojas's classic, makes textual comparisons of the two masterpieces and concludes that the *Celestina* not only closely follows the *Whip*'s style, but that several of its dialogues are directly inspired, indeed almost copied, from it. Moreover, Castro Guisasola, in his learned source study, finds that Martínez provided a great deal of material for the *Celestina.* And finally, Lida de Malkiel, although implicitly dismissing the Archpriest as an important source, preferring to seek precedents in classical works, almost grudgingly recognizes that he was nonetheless an influence.[16]

If we are to believe the 1501 edition's title page, the *Celestina* was "composed as a reprimand to mad lovers who, overcome by their excessive appetite, call their ladies God" (*compuesta en reprehensión de los locos enamorados, que vencidos en su desordenado apetito, a sus amigas llaman e dizen ser su Dios*).[17] Likewise, the *Whip*, whose subtitle is the disturbingly similar "reprobation of worldly love" (*reprobación del amor mundano*), rebukes those who pursue the course of mad love and adore their mistresses above the Creator. A cursory comparison of the preliminaries of both, then, reveals that their fundamental theme, purpose, and nature are apparently the same. Each in turn is an imprecation against lust and courtly love;[18] each views love as a blasphemous and diabolical instrument leading to man's downfall. However, apart from these general and indeed traditional considerations, the two bear a definite literary and stylistic relationship.

It is evident, for example, that more than one passage of the *Celestina* uses the *Whip* as its point of departure. As Puymaigre recognized as early as 1873, Sempronio's speech to Calisto exemplifying the great men who met their end through women can only be derived from the *Archpriest of Talavera.*[19] In it, the invitation to read about these exemplary men allows little speculation as to the immediate interdependency of the two passages. Moreover, in his admonition Sempronio cites Solomon, Seneca, Aristotle, and Bernardo as cases worthy of note; Calisto replies with Solomon, David, Aristotle, and Vergil. Of the figures in Calisto's retort, only Solomon and Aristotle are found in Sempronio's list, while David and Vergil are present in the *Whip*. This lack of concordance underlines the one passage's dependence on the other. The servant also recalls another ill-fated lover, Bernardo. This obscure reference can be to none other than Bernardo de Cabrera, an Aragonese courtier whose story is told to us by Martínez in Part I, Chapter 17, of his work.

Another allusion to the *Whip* immediately recognizable in the *Celestina* is Pármeno's well-known enumeration of the chemicals, occult trappings, and cosmetics found in the procuress's laboratory. And indeed, even the pejorative tone in which the young servant describes the lotions and brews Celestina purveys to the womenfolk of the town clearly evokes the Archpriest's equally famous censure of feminine vanity in the second part of his work.

Another echo of the *Archpriest of Talavera* is heard in Sempronio's infamous antifeminist diatribe. Bitterly summing up the moral inferiority of women, he lists their lies, traffickings, fickleness, lust, whimperings, mutability, arrogance, dissimulations, presumptuousness, vanity, chattering, lasciviousness, impudence, bewitchings, shamelessness, and pandering (just to name a few). The accusations in his speech are remarkably similar to the ones hurled by the Archpriest throughout Part II of his tract. Indeed one has only to glance at the chapter headings of the second part of the *Whip* to perceive this. Intent upon savagely denigrating women, both the *Celestina* and the *Archpriest of Talavera* are extraordinarily similar examples of fifteenth-century Castilian misogyny. Even the qualification with which Sempronio initiates his philippic—the fact that there are virtuous and noble women but that he will speak only of the bad ones—recalls the manner in which Martínez begins Part II of his work.

The influence of the *Archpriest of Talavera* on the *Celestina* is noticeable in additional thematic parallels. Both depict the commission of the seven deadly sins and the transgression of the Decalogue. The Archpriest at the outset of his work declares that "he who loves transgresses the Ten Commandments and commits all seven of the deadly sins" (61), and from this point until the end of Part I he exemplifies his statement. As Dorothy Clotelle Clarke confirms, the *Whip* has "two fundamental similarities that would indicate common purpose with the *Comedia*: the subject of carnal love, and the incorporation in the work of a conspicuous and lengthy sin list in such a way as to demonstrate that the commission of the seven sins (and . . . the breaking of God's Commandments also) is a direct consequence of carnal love. Although the . . . archpriest's technique differs greatly . . . the intended lesson is the same in the two works."[20]

Perhaps the most easily recognized point of connection between Rojas's masterpiece and the *Whip* is the figure of Celestina herself. Martínez's generic description of a procuress in Part II is most likely based on Trotaconventos of the *Book of Good Love*. And while it is possible that the creator of Celestina was inspired directly by Juan Ruiz, it is unlikely since a comparison of the qualities of his go-between shows that they parallel more closely the ones described in our author's work. The author of the anonymous first act of the *Celestina*, then, saw his character through the eyes of Alfonso Martínez. The bawd in the *Whip*, apart from being a procuress like Trotaconventos, is an erstwhile prostitute, an abortionist, a sorceress, and a corrupter of "matrons, widows, nuns, and even the betrothed" (157).

Apart from the motifs shared by both masterpieces, there is also a stylistic similarity that cannot be ignored. Martínez forged the verbal instrument that paved the way for the *Celestina* and is, in the words of Menéndez y Pelayo, "Rojas' most immediate precursor."[21] The realistic, rapid, direct dialogues and monologues we find in the *Whip* are one of its principal contributions to the later work. Although Stephen Gilman attempts to point out differences between the *Celestina*'s dialogic quality and the *Whip*'s, commenting that the characters in the latter's dialogues have no awareness of the person to whom they are supposed to be speaking and that they therefore possess a "style without perspective radiating from the sentiment of a single life,"[22] he overlooks the essence of Martínez's monologues. The Archpriest's monologues assume, indeed require, the character's awareness of each other (see Chapter 3, section II, of this study).

The dramatic technique of the *Celestina*, then, is found in its germinal form in Martínez's work. In his dialogues, but most especially his monologues, he conveys a vivid awareness of the *other* at times comparable in intensity and life to that of the *Celestina*. Although his characters' speeches at first seem to lack perspective, they surge forth from the affective opposition of two conflicting wills. As in the *Celestina*, the fervent interjections, complaints, and commands of the woman who lost the egg in our earlier example evoke and describe things and people beyond the work itself.

Rhetorically, the *Whip* and the *Celestina* conform on many points. Both, for example, exploit a mixed style, incorporating popular as well as learned modes of expression. As Carmelo Samonà observes in his study of rhetoric in the later work, "upon putting his hand to the *Celestina*, Rojas found himself in contact with two types of language—one rhetorical, the other popular—both filtered through the literary experiment of the Archpriest of Talavera."[23] Indeed, the *Celestina*'s incessant use of proverbs and colloquial speech mixed with cultivated imagery and diction forcefully brings to mind Martínez's hybrid preaching style in which the language of the people and the erudite parlance of the university merge to form an artistic unity without precedent in Castilian prose.

There are other mutual and even more specific characteristics of style in both works. Like the *Archpriest of Talavera*, the *Celestina* (especially in the first act) tends to use infinitive constructions in a Latinate manner, employs rhymed prose, an abundance of exclamations, rhetorical questions, and long enumerations of essentially synonymous nouns, verbs, and adjectives. All of these are seen by Samonà as "a sure derivative of the same procedures of the Archpriest of Talavera."[24]

II *The* Whip *Beyond the Fifteenth Century*

Even though five editions of the *Whip* from the sixteenth century survive, its most profound influence was understandably exerted upon works of the previous century. There are, however, several later important authors who, although not directly dependent upon Martínez's work, nevertheless betray an affinity for his innovative expressiveness and way of looking at the world. Antonio de Guevara, Francisco Delicado, and Miguel de Cervantes are all literary kindred spirits of the Archpriest.

Fray Antonio de Guevara (1480–1545), Bishop of Mondoñedo, is an author whose artistic abilities are only now beginning to be appreciated. An extremely influential and well-known writer in sixteenth-century Europe, he is credited by one scholar with inspiring the euphuistic movement in English literature.[25] While it is indeed likely that Guevara's style is the precursor of euphuism, showing a propensity for an excessive use of antitheses, alliterations, and obscure allusions to historical and mythological personages, it nonetheless contains a spontaneous idiomatic sensibility that makes use of "an undignified and unpolished lexicon . . . when it is not outright vulgar and colloquial."[26] It is in this decidedly dialectical mode of expression that Guevara most resembles Alfonso Martínez.

Von Richthofen claims that the didactic latinizing aspect of the *Whip*'s style contributed nothing to later Spanish literature.[27] Surely the German scholar has overlooked Antonio de Guevara. Guevara's use of a very personal, elegant, complicated, periodic Latinate style in conjunction with a well-defined colloquial element in his didactic works underscores his debt to Martínez. Furthermore, concrete stylistic characteristics like rhyming prose, antithesis, paranomasia, constant digressions, exclamations, interrogatives, and wordplay are integral notes of both these authors' expressiveness.[28] However, since Guevara makes no clear reference to Martínez or any of his works, a direct relationship is difficult to prove. Still, such a strong likeness exists between the two that to ignore it would be a disservice to both of them.

The most fundamental yet common characteristic shared by Guevara and Martínez is the nature of their didacticism: each writes with the preacher's acute sense of the likes and dislikes of his audience. The essence of their moralistic art is the not uncommon desire to teach while entertaining. The goal, granted, is inherent to all didactic works, but the methods used to achieve it are very similar in the Archpriest and Fray Antonio. Like Martínez, Guevara uses irony and satire as the vehicle for his entertaining lesson, expressing a point of view that sometimes descends to a low-life, picaresque level. While neither is the author of a picaresque novel, each displays a fondness for the antiheroic vision and characters that predates the jaundiced observations and personalities commonly associated with that genre. Sketches of underworld as well as commonplace characters abound in Guevara's *Menosprecio de corte y alabanza de aldea* (*In Reproach of the Court and in Praise of Country Life*) as they do in the *Whip*. Guevara's go-betweens are more than reminiscent of the bawds described in Martínez's work: "There is another type of evil people in the Capital, not men but women; women who have had their harvest and are very old and rancid from it. They serve as go-betweens and covers for hookers; to wit, they deceive nieces, suborn daughters-in-law, persuade neighbors, and pester sisters-in-law, sell their own daughters and, if not that, raise young girls for their purposes. The result of which, I say with tears in my eyes, is that they often have more lasses in their houses than eels in the plaza on market day."[29] Moreover, Guevara, like the Archpriest, "flings himself . . . into joyously depicting feminine weaknesses,"[30] criticizing women for their excessive use of cosmetics, the vanity of their clothes, their caprices, and their lack of better judgment.

The two artists are virtuosos of realistic description, meticulously delineating and often exaggerating even the most insignificant details. The Struggle of Poverty and Fortune in the *Whip*, for instance, is as rich in exploiting reality as Guevara's version of Christ's Passion in his *Monte Calvario* (*Mount Calvary*). In this work, the crucifixion of Jesus is depicted with almost savage verisimilitude that recalls Martínez's fondness for the grotesque: "The left hand securely nailed, they attempted to nail the right one but were unable to. . . . Once the excessive pain of the first spike had passed, the other arm was moved back and forth in an effort to align it with the bored hole the nail was to pass through. The hand fell three fingers short of the spot, however. They thus pulled the right arm and made it align with the hole. While they did this, they were sure to hold on to the already secured left arm so it would not tear away from the nail. Thus they first dismembered Jesus, then they nailed him."[31] Even the shape and size of the nail is dwelt upon: "long and thick and square and blunt."

An effort to infuse their respective sources with lifelike detail, to create the illusion of reality, is the artistic touchstone of Guevara and Martínez. Each is spurred on by the need to capture and hold the attention of his reader "through the means of familiar, quotidian things and descriptions."[32] Both create by examining the everyday events, evoking scenes, characters, situations, and dialogues observed in the plazas and marketplaces of fifteenth- and sixteenth-century Castile. Martínez and Guevara are fascinated by human conduct as well as by the physical world; they are literary sociologists who re-create and experiment with both people and their surroundings.

Accordingly, even the generic nature of their works is related, for each author sits centaurlike, to borrow an image from the late Professor Américo Castro, over literary creations that are not wholly essays or novels but contain the best elements of both. The *Reproach of the Court*, like the *Whip*, is dominated by the overpowering first person of its author, underscoring its affinity to the essay. Yet, the following scene with its enumeration of visual images brings to mind the fictional narrative and Martínez's occasional torrents of descriptive elements: "there is another type of damned good-for-nothings in the Capital. These are not received at court or at the monasteries, but wander through the inns, bars, and boarding houses and offer their services to majordomos, wine stewards, or the cook. From which it follows that what is the right of one is booty for the next; from the leftovers of the table and that which is put away, they always have sufficient to eat and sometimes they even carry bread in their shirts next to their chests."[33] The incidental detail, the passing idiosyncrasy which we have already discussed in the *Archpriest of Talavera*, betrays Guevara's inclination for novelistic devices. His rogues, as Lazarillo later does, take care to carry what extra food they can acquire inside their shirts. The exacting observation, the love of the revealing, graphic particular is a common bond tying the art of Antonio de Guevara to that of Alfonso Martínez.

The literary personality of both these authors is formed by, and firmly rooted in, the inherent paradox of the medieval pulpit—the necessity to morally instruct while at the same time entertain or shock.[34] Their respective works, even for the modern reader, are enjoyable lessons in Christian ethics which display a great similarity of style, themes, and vision. And, while it is still uncertain whether Guevara was directly familiar with Martinez's work, he shares with him a closely allied artistic spirit.

Another sixteenth-century writer displaying artistic similarities with Martínez de Toledo is Francisco Delicado, author of *La lozana andaluza* (*Exuberant Andalusian Women*), 1527, and a Spanish expatriate who spent the greater part of his life in Italy.[35] Delicado expresses views on women similar to Martínez's and was doubtless his disciple in the art of literary portraiture. In the *Andalusian Woman*, the vehicles of dialogue and monologue so effectively used by Martínez are developed to their maximum potential as an instrument of characterization. Through direct speech, characters are individualized and their expressions and feelings are captured by Delicado in order to convey a spontaneity and intimacy to the situations he portrays. Moreover, the scenes painted by this author are motivated by the same desire as those of Martínez—principally, the reprobation of lust. The *Andalusian Woman* is a didactic work aimed at correcting the moral lassitude, particularly sexual promiscuity, of the Roman Hispanic community at the beginning of the sixteenth century. As in the *Whip*, narrative dialogue is used to satirically undermine customs, people, and the everyday world in order to emphasize their viciousness. By laughing with Delicado, as with Martínez, we are able to perceive human error and attempt to correct it. In short, they both take a similar approach in presenting their moral.

As we have mentioned, woman plays a fundamental role in the *Andalusian Woman*, and Delicado perhaps looked to the

Whip as one of the many literary models for the misogynistic spirit he conveys. In his work, as in our author's, woman's grasping ambitiousness, her vanity (represented by her excessive use of cosmetics), and her inherent lustful nature are shown as the cause of man's perdition. Noting the similarities of both, Bruno Damiani observes that "Lozana and other courtesans in Delicado's work become that symbol of pride, greed, and deception which typifies women of *Corbacho* [the *Whip*]."[36] Nevertheless, although scornful and wary of woman, Delicado does not project Martínez's sustained intransigence toward her. In fact, Lozana, his principal character who in the end repents of her whoring ways, is praised in the book's Apology as a woman who "was vigilant in avoiding doing those things which were offensive to God and His Commandments."[37]

It is in the style and especially the point of view that Martínez's presence in the *Andalusian Woman* is most forcefully felt. The Archpriest doubtless offered Delicado a precedent for the witness-narrator motif in his work, because he becomes as much character as author when emphasizing the value of personal experience. Like Martínez, he adopts the posture of the worldly-wise moralist who insists upon telling what he has seen in order to buttress the meaning of his lesson and bring to life the vice and degradation he portrays. Moreover, this perspective contributes to a structural similarity between the two works in that colloquial dialogues of characters exemplifying sin alternate with the direct moralizing narrative of the author. In his style, the narrator is sure to dissociate himself from his characters, who generally speak in accordance with their inferior ethical and social makeup. Furthermore, in the moralistic sections of his work, such as the "Letter Added by the Author," Delicado resorts to the exclamatory and interrogative didactic preaching style employed by Martínez when he wished to draw attention to the lesson communicated in his exempla.

Delicado's *Andalusian Woman*, then, reflects one more trace of Alfonso Martínez's contribution to the Spanish literary heritage. It is a work that adopts the verbal instrument of popular speech introduced by our author in the previous century and uses it to create complex satirical literary portraits aimed at correcting vice and the folly of lust. Delicado adopts Martínez's techniques and brings them together in such a manner that they become the integrated components of a fully developed work of art. While the *Whip* remains more essay than novel, the *Andalusian Woman* fulfills its novelistic potentials and brings many of Martínez's innovations to fruition.

Although there is no sure indication that Miguel de Cervantes knew the *Whip*, Menéndez y Pelayo singles out his *Don Quijote* as one more of its literary heirs. Alfonso Martínez, he tells us, is Cervantes' progenitor in "the felicitous use of proverbs and adagia that contribute such an exquisitely pure-blooded Castilian [*castizo*] quality . . . to the dialogues of the *Quijote*."[38] Likewise, Helmut Hatzfeld acknowledges Cervantes' possible debt to our author, noting that both exploit indecorous conduct as a means of characterization as well as popular comparisons, metaphors, and figures of speech that stand out because of their vividness and suggestiveness.[39] Professor Hatzfeld also feels that Martínez is Cervantes' only notable predecessor in the Spanish tradition capable of creating direct pictorial images and accurate, lifelike descriptions of gestures.[40] Indeed, these two authors are masters of pictorial literature especially accomplished at describing tumultuous scenes full of movement and action evoked through the deliberate use of verbal accumulations and prolonged series of terse sentences.[41]

While it is quite possible *Don Quijote*'s picturesque descriptions of habits and gestures could reveal an influence from the *Whip*, it is nevertheless difficult to determine for certain, since Cervantes was well versed in Italian literature and a connoiseur of Boccaccio, Bandello, and other *novellieri* whose works abound in graphic evocations of the everyday. The use of colloquial and sententious speech, however, is another matter. Although Cervantes' predilection for proverbs and folk idioms is typically Renaissance and acquired through his humanistic formation (Erasmus and Juan de Mal Lara in particular),[42] there are several curious proverbs in *Don Quijote* and the *Whip*, along with some other stylistic elements, that might reflect the influence of the one work upon the other. The motivation for Cervantes' use of adagia and colloquialisms can be traced to the Neo-Platonic belief that they express man's immanent morality,[43] as opposed to Martínez's traditional aphoristic didacticism. This notwithstanding, many of the proverbial sayings we find in the *Archpriest of Talavera* appear in the later masterwork. The following are just a few examples: "Silent discretion is called Sancho" (*Que al buen callar llaman Sancho*); "When they give you a goat, hurry with the rope" (*Quando te dieren la cabrilla, acorre con la soguilla*); "The dog donned hunting breeches and no longer recognized his companion" (*Vídose el perro en bragas de çerro; non conosçió a su conpañero*).[44]

Following Hatzfeld's initiative, von Richthofen attempts to substantiate *Don Quijote*'s stylistic debt to the *Whip* and concludes that "in his use of sententiae, accumulations, antitheses, exclamations, and word-play Cervantes was not uninfluenced by the work of Alfonso Martínez."[45] Nevertheless, the stylistic and paroemiological analogies drawn by this critic fail to unequivocally establish the relationship of the two. That is to say, there are no allusions or textual parallels that definitely confirm Cervantes' familiarity with our author's work. This notwithstanding, von Richthofen's examples point at the very least to a subjective kinship of both artists. Through them, although we cannot perceive direct influences, we can appreciate how in a roundabout manner Martínez's *Whip* in the mid-fifteenth century announced the future direction of the mainstream of Spanish prose.

Briefly, then, Cervantes and Martínez are united by a certain although distant literary relationship. Some of the Archpriest's proverbs and elements of his style resurface in *Don Quijote*, adding to this work's humor and artistic brilliance. If Martínez did not directly influence Cervantes, he at least pointed the way, providing one of the basic points of departure leading to the creation of the modern novel.

CHAPTER 7

Hagiographer and Historian

ALTHOUGH Martínez de Toledo is best known as the creator of the *Whip*, he was nonetheless author of several other works of lesser renown. These were all composed after his celebrated masterpiece and attest to the versatility of his literary talents and the variety of his interests.

I *Hagiographies and Translations*

The writing of saints' lives was one of the principal literary occupations of the Middle Ages. Indeed, there is scarcely a saint who did not have his biography written during this period; and there is scarcely an author who did not have his favorite saint to write about. Martínez de Toledo revered two holy men—San Ildefonso and San Isidoro—and chose to chronicle their lives as examples to others.

The Archpriest's *Vida de San Ildefonso* (*Life of San Ildefonso*), 1444, tells the life history of Ildefonso, Archbishop of Toledo from 657 to 667. It is divided into eighteen brief, chronologically arranged chapters. A typical medieval hagiography, it begins by describing the saint's family background, noting that he was the nephew of San Eugenio, prelate of Toledo (636–646). The marriage of his father, don Esteban, and his mother, doña Lucía, was initially childless. A pious woman especially devoted to the Virgin, doña Lucía prayed that she might have a child. In a dream, the Holy Mother came to her and announced the future birth of a son who would remain in the service of the Virgin throughout his life. As promised, a male child was born and christened Ildefonso. His first spoken words were the Hail Mary. A precocious child, at twelve he was sent to study with Saint Isidore in Seville.

Under Isidore's tutelage Ildefonso proved himself an outstanding student whose continued devotion to the Virgin was of particular note. After learning the "science" of theology, Ildefonso returned to Toledo in order to teach. Impressed with his knowledge and piety, San Eugenio conferred priesthood upon him and rewarded him with the archdeaconry of the city. Nevertheless, much to the chagrin of his father, Ildefonso shunned his appointment because it was too worldly. Instead, he preferred to enter the cloister. His father's anger was assuaged by his mother's good reasoning and her prayers to the Virgin. In time the young monk was elected abbot of his monastery despite his protestations that he was unworthy. As head of this community he was exemplary.

Ildefonso's father died, but not before he was inspired to do good works in the name of God. Later, doña Lucía was visited by the Holy Mother on her deathbed and assured of her own salvation. In a vision, Mary informed Ildefonso of his mother's passing. With the inheritance from his parents he founded a nearby convent. When his uncle, the bishop, died, he was elected Archbishop of Toledo since the clergy was agreed there was no holier man in Spain.

Meanwhile, Satan fomented trouble and consternation. The teachings of Helvidius began to circulate in Toledo. This heresiarch taught that after the virgin birth of Jesus Mary begat other children with Joseph. Recognizing the enormity of this error, Ildefonso wrote his *De Virginitate Sanctae Mariae Contra Tres Infideles* (*On the Virginity of Saint Mary and Directed Against Three Infidels*). In thanks, the Virgin appeared to him and promised to watch over him in life as in death. In order to eradicate completely Helvidius's heresey, Ildefonso called a council. There he ratified the virginity of Mary and instituted a national feast in her honor. Shortly thereafter, and in the presence of the king, Ildefonso was celebrating a mass in honor of Santa Leocadia. During the ceremony Leocadia rose from her sepulcher and thanked the archbishop for his works on behalf of the Holy Mother. This, however, was just the beginning. At the celebration of the first mass of the new feast in honor of Mary, the Virgin appeared to Ildefonso and presented him with a gift from Her son—a miraculous chasuble direct from the vaults of heaven. It was made expressly for Ildefonso, and whosoever wore it other than he would instantly die.

After nine years as archbishop, Ildefonso died from a great fever—not, of course, without first having put his affairs in order and having admonished his fellow priests to live a virtuous life. At the moment of his death the room filled with light and he was heard conversing with Saint Mary. When the soul left the flesh, the latter took on a crystallike appearance and, rather than corrupt, gave off a pleasing fragrance. Many miracles were performed upon those who viewed the body. After three days Ildefonso was buried amid great pomp and solemnity.

Sergio was elected the new Archbishop of Toledo, but he was not Ildefonso's peer. In fact, he was a proud, vain man who envied his predecessor. One day, he ordered the heavenly chasuble brought to him so that he might wear it. The moment he put it on, it began to squeeze in upon him until he burst. From that day forward no one dared wear the vestment.

From the literary point of view, the *Life of San Ildefonso* can hardly be called significant or original. In fact, its modern editor, José Madoz y Moleres, even uses the word "paraphrase" to characterize it.[1] That is to say, it is intimately and primarily based upon a Latin biography of the saint written in 1308, the *Legenda B. Ildephonsi Archiepiscopi Toletani* (*Legend of the Beatific Ildephonsus, Archbishop of Toledo*). In addition to this source, however, Martínez's familiarity with other works dealing with the saint's life is also noticeable. This is the case with San Julián de Toledo's (d. 690) *Beati Ildefonsi Elogium* (*In Praise of the Beatific Ildephonsus*), Bishop Cixila's (d. 783) *Vita vel Gesta S. Ildephonsi Toletanae* (*Life or Deeds of Saint Ildephonsus of Toledo*), and Rodrigo Manuel Cerratense's *Vita Beati Ildephonsi Archiepiscopi Toletani* (*Life of the Beatific Ildephonsus, Archbishop of Toledo*).[2] A close relationship with Beneficiado de Úbeda's vernacular poem, the *Vida de San Ildefonso* (*Life of San Ildefonso*), ca. 1300, is also evident.[3]

Despite the pronounced dependency of the *Life of San Ildefonso* on its sources, Martínez does occasionally modify the material he draws upon. Of particular significance is his ability to organize events into a plot and weed out the real from the purely legendary. Of all Ildefonso's hagiographies Martínez's is the one most faithful to the facts. This, of course, is not to say that it is historical—it revels in the saint's miracles—but that it provides perhaps the most accurate and well-organized account of his life as told by his medieval biographers.

The Archpriest's irrepressible fondness for literary elaboration is also evident in the work. In order to personalize the narrative he often uses the free indirect style, entering his characters' minds and reproducing their thoughts and words. This interest in personality lends a dramatic intimacy and picturesqueness to the otherwise unexciting hagiography. And, as in the *Whip*, an important dimension of this work is local color. Anachronistically, the saint speaks and acts like a fifteenth-century Castilian prelate. His actions, customs, and milieu are all more appropriate to the court of Juan II than to seventh-century Visigothic Spain. After studying in Seville, for example, Ildefonso returns home proudly proclaiming to his parents that San Isidoro gave "me my Master's Degree in Holy Theology."[4] Master's degrees were, of course, a product of late medieval universities, so this scene, and others like it, adds a rather quaint touch to the work. In short, the *Life of San Ildefonso*, although not terribly original, does possess its literary merits.

The Archpriest must have felt particular empathy for San Ildefonso. Not only did he bear the saint's name (Alfonso is a variant of Ildefonso) and come from the same city, he even possessed benefices the holy man was reputed to have held. At the time of his death Martínez was Archdeacon of Toledo, as we have seen, and he tells us that Ildefonso also held that office when he returned from Seville.[5] Moreover, both were fervent defenders of the Immaculate Conception and made it a point to leave written testimony of their devotion to the Virgin Mary. In fact, Martínez translated the saint's *On the Virginity of Saint Mary*, an ardent defense of this doctrine, and included it in the manuscript where his *Life of San Ildefonso* is found.[6]

Ildefonso's treatise is a particularly important work. It was one of the most widely circulated arguments in defense of the Immaculate Conception and brought him the great respect of Church historians.[7] The teachings of Jovinian and Helvidius, which Saint Jerome had reproached in his *Adversus Jovinianum* (*Against Jovinian*) and *Adversus Helvidium* (*Against Helvidius*), angered Ildefonso and motivated him to write the work. According to José Madoz y Moleres, however, it is not simply an attack against long dead heresiarchs but a response to the immediate theological climate of seventh-century Toledo. Madoz believes the saint wrote his defense of the virginity of Mary in order to combat the assaults on the doctrine by Toledan Jews.[8] This is likely just a rhetorical posture, however, for the three figures against whom the treatise is directed (Jovinian, Helvidius, and a Jew) represent the three major opponents of the Immaculate Conception.

Ildefonso's work is thus aimed against the three principal unbelievers in the Immaculate Conception. Divided into ten chapters with a prologue, it is a masterpiece of theological invective. Essentially, there are three parts to the work. The first part is a defense of the virgin birth refuting Jovinian, who accepted Mary's virginity at conception but not after. The second part is aimed at Helvidius, who maintained that after Jesus, Mary conceived other children with Joseph. The third, last, and longest part (seven chapters in length) speaks to the Jew and defends the *perpetual* virginity of Mary.

Rather than in its doctrinal content, however, the work's chief importance lies in its style. Throughout the Middle Ages there was a continuing stylistic imitation of it. María Rosa Lida briefly studies its contribution to medieval and Renaissance expression and concludes that its contrasts, short periods, and abundant use of synonyms were instrumental in the development of early essayistic vernacular literature.[9]

Martínez's translation of this opuscule is masterful. It faithfully renders the *more synonymorum* ("synonymic manner") of the original and thus represents one of the major documents to introduce this elegant Latinate style into the vernacular. Primarily a diatribe and an exercise in stylistic virtuosity, then, it is testimony to his facility with language, knowledge of Latin, and consciousness of style. Moreover, it confirms his preoccupation with formal rhetoric and establishes him as one of the leading figures in the early Castilian essay. *De la virginidat de Nuestra Señora* (*On the Virginity of Our Lady*) reveals the Archpriest's sensibility to the artificiality of rhetoric and represents one of the first and therefore main attempts to identify Spanish prose with Latin. Its cadences, tropes, and other stylistic elements all define it as a touchstone in the development of Castilian expository writing. It anticipates by a full fifty years incipient humanism's deliberate desire to make Castilian sound and seem like Latin.[10] Hence, our author's translation is a fundamental conduit by which the rhetorical modes of Latin were introduced into the early Spanish essay.

There are three extant manuscripts of the Archpriest's *Life of San Ildefonso* and *On the Virginity of Our Lady*: codex number 11 of the Menéndez y Pelayo Library (*S*) in Santander; Castilian codex b.III.1 of the Escurial Library (*E*); and codex 1.178 of the Biblioteca Nacional in Madrid (*M*). In addition to the treatise on the Immaculate Conception and Ildefonso's biography, *M* and *E* also contain a *Vida de Sanct Isidoro* (*Life of San Isidoro*) attributable to Martínez de Toledo. *E*'s first person explicit (folio 131v) identifies the three works as belonging to our author and seems to indicate that he wrote them as an act of penitence for some transgression. It reads as follows: "Thus, I, Alfonso Martínez of Talavera, unworthy sinner, unmindful archpriest, lacking the fervor that I should and am obliged to have toward the Holy Virgin, this uncorrupted Mother of God, made and wrote the present treatise on account of my sins and misdemeanors."

His *Life of San Isidoro* is divided into thirty-one chapters and a prologue. Like the *Life of San Ildefonso* it follows a chronological order, but is not as well organized with regard to continuity. The prologue, a panegyric of the saint said to have been written by one of his contemporaries, repeatedly compares him to Saint James. From childhood Isidoro showed evidence of being an extraordinary person. He was very inquisitive, according to the legend, and after receiving lessons from his older brother, he wrote to Gregory the Great and impressed him with his knowledge. Miraculously, Isidoro was transported to Rome, where he met with Gregory. Upon his return to Spain he is credited with crushing all the heresies of his time, especially the Arrian doctrine, and converting King Recarredo to Orthodox Catholicism.

When his brother and mentor, San Leandro, died, San Isidoro was elected bishop of Seville. As prelate he ensured the Faith's perpetuity in Spain while ardently defending the dogma of the Incarnation and the Holy Trinity. He is even said to have driven Mohammed from the peninsula when, as legend has it, he came to preach in Córdoba. Moreover, the miracles Isidoro performed in France, and his daily charity, are all chronicled.

Although the saint's secular writings are mentioned in the *Life of San Isidoro*, particular attention is paid to a spurious *Tractadello de la oración* (*Treatise on Prayer*). In fact, this *Treatise on Prayer* is Chapter XX of the hagiography. It is followed by a series of epistles (Chapters XXI–XXVI) between Isidoro and Mausona (Bishop of Mérida), Braulio (Bishop of Zaragoza), San Eugenio (Archbishop of Toledo), and Leofredo (Bishop of Córdoba). After this interruption, the narrative is taken up once again and we are told how Isidoro defeated a heretic in public debate; how, possessing the gift of prophecy, he predicted his own death; how before dying he called a Church council to reassert and ensure the continued belief in the Trinity in Spain; and how after confessing, communing, and giving his worldly goods to charity, he finally died. As in the *Life of San Ildefonso,* the corpse failed to corrupt and performed miracles upon those who came to view it. The body was laid to rest with his two siblings, San Leandro and Santa Florentina. Even after death, however, San Isidoro performed miracles and always inspired warm devotion from the kings of Spain—especially Juan II, who always carried his standard in battle.

If the *Life of San Ildefonso* paraphrases its sources, the *Life of San Isidoro* is little more than a translation of them. Indeed, as Madoz y Moleres points out, it is probably a translation of a Latin manuscript (27,28 of the Biblioteca Nacional, Fondo de Toledo, Madrid) containing a *Vita Sancti Isidori* (*Life of San Isidoro*) attributed to Lucas of Tuy.[11] Nevertheless, Martínez does edit the original slightly, synthesizing episodes diffused throughout the Tudense's Latin version while adding some of his own considerations to the narrative. Furthermore, he also relies on certain other sources to confirm and complete his hagiography.

Chapter X, for example, is based on Chapter XXVI of Lucas de Tuy's *Chronicon Mundi* (*World Chronicle*). Moreover, the first half of Chapter XXX relies on another of the Tudense's works, *De Altera Vita* (*On the Other Life*), while later the *Crónica de Juan II* (*Juan II's Chronicle*) and Rodrigo Jiménez de Rada's *De Rebus Hispaniae* (*Concerning the Things of Spain*) are mentioned. Allusions to printing (not introduced into the peninsula until the mid-1470s) and printed works in the last chapters of the *Life of San Isidoro* indicate that the Archpriest's translation was itself retouched sometime late in the fifteenth century, probably by Alvar Gómez, the amanuensis of the manuscript. As with his *On the Virginity of Our Lady*, Martínez's translation is notable for its fidelity to the original text and his ability to render the stylistic nuances of Latin into Castilian. And, like the *Life of San Ildefonso*, this hagiography also contains many anachronisms, although they can be found in the Latin parent text.

II *Historian*

Martínez's literary endeavors, then, were not limited to the *Whip*. After completion of this work, he maintained a continued interest in writing and translation. However, had he never written his masterwork or his hagiographies, he would still merit a prominent place in the history of Spanish literature as the author of *La atalaya de las crónicas* (*Watchtower of the Chronicles*). Martínez's most extensive work, and the one he devoted the greatest amount of attention to, it was composed, according to Diego de Colmenares, the seventeenth-century historian, at the behest of Juan II.[12] Still unpublished, the *Watchtower of the Chronicles* is one of the most important documents of medieval Spanish historiography.

There are eight surviving manuscripts of the *Watchtower*, a fact that attests its importance and popularity. In an exhaustive study of the manuscript tradition, however, Raúl A. del Piero has determined that only five of the eight codices are critically important; the rest are later copies of these.[13] The fundamental texts, then, are *P*, Biblioteca del Placio de Oriente (Madrid) ms. 1892; *V*, codex Palatinus Vindibonensis Hispanicus (Vienna) no. 3424*; *H*, Academia de la Historia (Madrid) ms. 26–1–21; *E*, Castilian codex X.i.12 of the Escurial Library (folios 312r–398v); and finally *L*, codex Egerton (British Museum) no. 287.

L is the most accurate and complete. *P*, *V*, *H*, and *E* end in the midst of the history of King Enrique III, while *L*, representing an independent branch of the tradition, continues the narrative up through the reign of Juan II to the death of Alvaro de Luna.

The work was begun by Martínez in 1443, as he tells us in several places throughout the text. Therefore, it must have been ten years in the writing since it ends with Luna's execution, an event that occurred in 1453. The most complete version of the text (*L*) is composed of sixty-eight chapters. The first two form an introduction relating the origin and migrations of the Goths to Spain and tell of the reign of King Walia. From the end of Chapter II until the end of the work, each succeeding chapter recounts the history of one of the kings of Spain. There is only one exception, Chapter XVI, which relates the story of Mohammed.[14] This is the only part of the narrative taking place outside the peninsula, although Martínez (as in Chapter XVII of his *Life of San Isidoro*) retells the legend whereby the Prophet came to preach in Córdoba. This short history of Mohammed was doubtless added by our author in order to explain the Moslem invasion in the ensuing sketch of King Recarred's reign (Chapter XVII) and once again attests to his preoccupation with the logical organization of his work.

Martínez makes his purpose known in the prologue:

> I have proposed and endeavored to compile the deeds of as many kings as possible, Goths, Spaniards, and Castilians alike. This according to the chronicles to which I have had access; taking from these the conclusions of bygone Spanish events so as to freshen the memories of those who have in the past read and might have forgotten them. . . . Hence we arrive at my ultimate purpose: writing a bit about the facts pertaining to Spain, because I know there are many who take pleasure in reading of the deeds of our forebears, especially those who are deserving of remembrance for their admirable and loyal actions. I do this in the hope that my readers' spirits might be fortified by the things I tell.[15]

In short, the Archpriest attempts to provide a practical concise history of Spain compiled from as many sources as were available to him. This in itself makes the *Watchtower* a unique work, for it imposes very modern criteria on the art of writing history. In the first place, it seeks to be primarily informative, more of an encyclopedic reference source of history than a chronicle in the medieval sense of the word. Moreover, this objective automatically subjects Martínez to a process of selectivity. His desire for brevity dictates that he must choose from his sources only those things he deems important. What he offers in his *Watchtower of the Chronicles,* then, is one of Spain's first endeavors at writing modern textbook history. Through research, he selects, digests, retells, and interprets the Spanish past in order to make it more accessible to the general reading public. As the title implies, the *Watchtower of the Chronicles* provides a panoramic overview of Spanish history by briefly surveying the major historical narratives written up until the middle of the fifteenth century.

The sources Martínez utilized in composing this work are not, however, as varied as he implies in his prologue. In fact, the events till the middle of the thirteenth century are almost solely derived from the *Primera crónica general* (*First General Chronicle*).[16] Nevertheless, this is very significant, since it makes Martínez the only fifteenth-century Castilian historian to make use of Alfonso the Learned's chronicle. Indeed, the relationship between the Archpriest's and Alfonso's work is often so close that it is even possible to determine which manuscript tradition of the *First General Chronicle* he used when preparing his text.[17]

The other sources employed are the *Crónica de 1344* (*Chronicle of 1344*), and the *Crónica de veinte reyes* (*Chronicle of Twenty Kings*). Although Fitzmaurice-Kelly and Sánchez Alonso claim there exists an overwhelming influence from Pedro del Corral's *Crónica sarracina* (*Saracen Chronicle*),[18] textual comparison with this work reveals that the *Watchtower* coincides with it on only one point—the description of Hercules' house in Toledo. Even then, as del Piero points out, when contrasted the two descriptions of this legendary house show a similarity that could be considered only general at best.[19] Instead of the *Saracen Chronicle*'s being an influence on our author, each passage is probably based upon a common source—a now lost reworking (*refundición*) of the *Crónica del moro Rasis* (*Chronicle of Rasis the Moor*).

Georges Cirot and Madeleine Pardo point out textual parallels between the last chapters of the *Watchtower* (from the reign of Enrique III onward, found only in *L*, folios cclviii ff.) and various other mid-fifteenth-century chronicles: Fernán Pérez de Guzmán's *Generaciones y semblanzas* (*Generations and Portraits*), an *Abreviación de la Crónica del halconero* (*Abbreviation of the Falconer's Chronicle*), and the *Anales de Garci Sánchez* (*Annals of Garci Sánchez*).[20] Whether these works influenced the *Watchtower* or vice versa is another matter. Relying on a passage mentioning the transference of Alvaro de Luna's remains from Valladolid to Toledo (the date of which is not known), Miss Pardo somewhat arbitrarily fixes this event in 1483 and, therefore, concludes that Martínez might not have been the author of these last chapters. As a result, she posits the influence of the chronicles we have mentioned upon a possible continuer of the work. Until a reliable chronological moment can be unequivocally established for the transference of Luna's remains to Toledo, however, her assertions can be neither affirmed nor denied. The only thing we may conclude is that the *Generations and Portraits*, the *Abbreviation of the Falconer's Chronicle*, and the *Annals of Garci Sánchez* all share textual similarities with the last chapters of the *Watchtower of the Chronicles*.

Martínez's stated desire for brevity leads him to sometimes summarize extensively. Indeed, on occasion this impulse is so strong that he condenses in a few words entire sections considered fundamental by the historians who composed his sources. The famous lament on Spain's loss to the Moors in the *First General Chronicle*,[21] an extremely well-known and lengthy passage, for instance, is reduced by Martínez to the following laconic statement: "Thus, when all had passed [the Moslem invasion], great was Spain's mourning; and great were the trials and tribulations suffered by all on account of Witiza's sinful carnality and that of don Rodrigo, his successor."[22]

On the other hand, however, the literary personality we saw in the *Whip* often breaks through and elaborates the sources in familiar ways. A clear example of this is evident if we compare the episode in the *First General Chronicle* recounting Fernán González's escape from prison with the help of doña Sancha and its version in the *Watchtower*. Chapter 711 of the earlier work relates an incident in which the count and the princess are forced to assassinate a lecherous archpriest in order to make good their flight. Their hiding place is discovered by the cleric's hunting dogs, whereupon he offers not to report their escape if doña Sancha sleeps with him. Faced with this proposition, she feigns consent and leads the archpriest on. In the meantime, the count comes up behind him and stabs him to death. They take his mule and escape.[23] Although a lengthy episode, Martínez's superior dramatic rendition of the incident deserves to be cited in its entirety:

The next day an archpriest—mind you, not the one from Talavera—while hunting with his dogs picked up their scent and flushed them out. When the archpriest saw them, he said: "Aha, where are you evildoers off to? So here you are! Just wait, I'm going to tell the king and I'll have you killed!" They begged him to have pity, and the count promised him and his heirs a city in Castile. He replied he'd have none of it. Then they said: "Well, what is your want?" The archpriest answered: "I won't do anything you ask me, nor will I be quiet unless she consents to lie with me." When the count heard this I know you can imagine how he felt, and he responded: "Friend, your petition is unjust. Ask for anything else and it will be given; but this, you yourself can see the wrong in it." He said: "Well, good-bye, I am off to the king." The count replied: "As you wish, good riddance!" The count enviously surveyed the mule the archpriest was riding. He thought how nice it would be to get his hands upon it, or, if not that, its owner. At this, the princess, as if moving to one side, said: "Wait, friend; wait just a moment." Noting the consequences of being discovered, she turned and said softly to the count: "I'll go off with him and grab him when he comes toward me, then you come up and kill him." The count said: "Madame, don't let go of him; and don't allow him to do anything upon your person." This she promised, and turning to the cleric said: "Friend, Archpriest, I've spoken with the count and he consents provided two conditions are met; that you shall never tell anyone of this; and that your wishes take place out of his sight, away from him." The archpriest, since he was evil, said in an evil tone: "That's what I want." Agreed, he went behind a bush not far away. The princess followed him, and in order to convince him took the reins of his mule and tied them to the bush. Then she turned and said: "Friend, let this be a secret unto God." He swore it would be. The archpriest disrobed and went toward her. She raised her arms as if to embrace him and then began to squeeze so tightly with her hands, teeth gnashing, that he couldn't get away. Meanwhile, still wearing his chains, the count, sometimes jumping, other times crawling, was struggling toward them. Thinking the rascal might get away, he wished it was all over while crying out: "Madame, hold on to him tight. I am coming." In the meantime, the princess and archpriest fell to the ground. She wouldn't let go even though she was being tossed around in the dirt amidst the barking dogs. Finally, the count grasped the archpriest, forced him to release his hold on the princess, and stabbed him repeatedly until he gave up the ghost. Then he tied the dogs together. They both mounted the mule sidesaddle and rode off with the dogs in tow to hide beneath some cliffs. (Codex Egerton, folios 108v–109v)

When compared to the Alfonsine version, Martínez's excels in its superior dramatism, characterization, and organization. In fact, it reminds us of the exuberant tumultuous scenes encountered in the *Whip*. The count and princess are more cautious, more calculating, more convincing, and, therefore, more human than the ones depicted in the *First General Chronicle*. Our author converts the scene into a psychological encounter in which he clearly delineates the steps by which the egotistical archpriest, moved by lust, throws caution to the wind and falls easy prey to the fleeing lovers. He also analyzes Fernán González's complex motivations for wishing the cleric dead: not only is the archpriest an immoral lecher in the count's eyes, but also the owner of a handsome mule that could facilitate the escape. It is not only righteousness, then, but common sense that inspires González to act.

The simultaneously pathetic and comical image of the count struggling and stumbling over his chains to reach the princess and her attacker; the princess tenaciously holding on while being knocked about in the dirt amid the barking dogs; the detail of tying the dogs together before departing; and the description of mounting the mule sidesaddle are all unique to the *Watchtower*. And all are Alfonso Martínez de Toledo's indelible hallmarks of literary realism. In short, while more often than not abbreviating his sources, the Archpriest also uses them as inspiration for dramatized scenes of great literary merit. His *Watchtower of the Chronicles*, then, is not only an important monument of fifteenth-century Spanish historiography, but also a noteworthy antecedent of the historical novel.

CHAPTER 8

Summation

IN the preceding chapters we have attempted to demonstrate Alfonso Martínez de Toledo's important contribution to the rise of the Spanish narrative. He was a man who lived in a revolutionary age and a man who wrote revolutionary literature. In him we witness one of those rare moments in the development of art—a transition. In many ways Martínez conveys medieval ideas: his preoccupation with orthodox morality; his heavy emphasis on Scholastic theology and reasoning; his dialectical vision of the world. In other ways he projects the image of an innovator: his sometimes unconscious intoxication with the creatures of his imagination; his interest in the human personality; his language, which communicates a clear picture of a situation and the immediacy of emotion; and his down-to-earth, realistic temperament that recognized that man's values were changing and would no longer tolerate the abstract allegorical didacticism of the medieval past.

Moreover, his work provides us with an invaluable social chronicle of fifteenth-century Castile. In reading his *Archpriest of Talavera*, or *Whip*, we are privy to the spoken idiom, the common events, the emotions, the total human comedy that immediately surrounded him. From another perspective, we are also offered one man's opinion of what is taking place: the righteous cleric who denounces the changing habits of his contemporaries with wit, pity, irony, and threats.

In fine, then: from the diversity, nature, and complexity of Alfonso Martínez de Toledo's artistic personality we may conclude that he was the most significant Castilian prose writer of the first half of the fifteenth century, and that as such, he contributed greatly to the development of both Spanish and European literature.

Notes and References

Chapter One

1. Marcelino Menéndez y Pelayo, *Poetas de la corte de don Juan II*, 2nd ed. (Buenos Aires: Espasa-Calpe, 1946), p. 12.
2. Julio Rodríguez-Puértolas, *Poesía de protesta en la Edad Media castellana* (Madrid: Gredos, 1968), p. 42.
3. Lesley Byrd Simpson, trans., *Little Sermons on Sin: The Archpriest of Talavera,* by Alfonso Martínez de Toledo (Berkeley: University of California Press, 1959), p. 9. Unless otherwise noted, all subsequent quotations from the work will be from this edition and page references will be given in the text.
4. Cristóbal Pérez Pastor, ed., *Arcipreste de Talavera (Corvacho o reprobación del amor mundano),* by Alfonso Martínez de Toledo, Sociedad de Bibliófilos Españoles, 35 (Madrid: Vda. de M. Tello, 1901, pp. xx–xxi.
5. *Ibid.*, pp. v–vi.
6. *Ibid.*, p. xvi.
7. Martín de Riquer, ed., *Arcipreste de Talavera,* by Alfonso Martínez de Toledo (Barcelona: Selecciones Bibliófilas, 1949), p. 9.
8. We wish to thank Professor Lomax for his generosity in providing us with a typescript of his still unpublished "Datos biográficos sobre el Arcipreste de Talavera," forthcoming in the *Actas del Congreso Internacional de Hispanistas* (Salamanca, for 1972). All further biographical facts followed by parentheses and *Bulario*, plus document number, are owed to Professor Lomax. They refer to his findings in Vicente Beltrán de Heredia, *Bulario de la Universidad de Salamanca (1219–1549)* (Salamanca: Universidad de Salamanca, 1966–67). Some of Lomax's conclusions are paralleled by Vicente Beltrán de Heredia in his *Cartulario de la Universidad de Salamanca* (Salamanca: Universidad de Salmanca, 1970), chapter 25.
9. Verardo García Rey, "El Arcipreste de Talavera, Alonso Martínez de Toledo," *Revista de la Biblioteca, Archivo, y Museo del Ayuntamiento de Madrid,* V (1928), 300.
10. This episode is in Part IV of the work, not included in Simpson's translation. It can be found in Joaquín González Muela, ed.,

Arcipreste de Talavera o Corbacho, by Alfonso Martínez de Toledo, Clásicos Castalia, 24 (Madrid: Castalia, 1970), pp. 238–43.

11. Pérez Pastor, p. vi.
12. *Ibid.*, pp. vii–viii.
13. José Madoz y Moleres, ed., *Vidas de San Ildefonso y San Isidoro*, by Alfonso Martínez de Toledo, Clásicos Castellanos, 134 (Madrid: Espasa-Calpe, 1962), p. 137.
14. Erich von Richthofen, "Alfonso Martínez de Toledo und sein *Arcipreste de Talauera*, ein kastilisches Prosawerk des 15. Jahrhunderts," *Zeitschrift für romanische Philologie*, LXI (1941), 426–27.
15. In describing the contents of the Fernández letter, Professor Lomax uses the word *casado* ("married").
16. García Rey, p. 301.
17. Archivo Histórico Nacional, Clero, carpeta 2979, document 14.
18. Simpson, p. 4.
19. Pérez Pastor, p. xxiv.
20. García Rey, p. 302.
21. *Ibid.*, pp. 302–303.

Chapter Two

1. Anna Krause, "Further Remarks on the Archpriest of Talavera," *Bulletin of Spanish Studies*, VI (1929), 57.
2. Erich von Richthofen, "Alfonso Martínez de Toledo und sein *Arcipreste de Talauera*," pp. 458–61.
3. Mario Penna, ed., *Arcipreste de Talavera*, by Alfonso Martínez de Toledo (Torino: Rosenberg and Sellier, 1955), p. xl.
4. The manuscript consists of 107 foliated leaves, two columns of fifteenth-century courtly caligraphy (*letra cortesana*) per page, written in ink with Arabic numeral pagination 280 × 193 mm. See Julián Zarco Cuevas, *Catálogo de los manuscritos castellanos de la Real Biblioteca del Escorial* (Madrid: Helénica, 1924), I, 220–21.
5. Penna, p. lii. See also Cuevas, I, 220; von Richthofen, 437; and José Simón Díaz, *Bibliografía de la literatura hispánica,* 2nd ed. (Madrid: CSIC, 1960–65), III, 2, 364.
6. Konrad Haebler, *Bibliografía ibérica del siglo XV* (The Hague and Leipzig: Nijhoff, 1903), I, 192, no. 404.
7. For a complete description of the incunabula see Penna, pp. li–lvi.
8. *Ibid.*, p. lvi.
9. Von Richthofen, p. 441.
10. *Ibid.*, p. 470.
11. Penna, p. 80, note.

12. See Théodore Joseph Boudet, Comte de Puymaigre, *La Cour littéraire de don Juan II* (Paris: A. Franck, 1873), I, 156–65; also, José Amador de los Ríos, *Historia crítica de la literatura española* (Madrid: Fernández Cancela, 1865), VI, 277–85; and Cristóbal Pérez Pastor, ed., *Arcipreste de Talavera.*

13. Christine J. Whitbourn, *The "Arcipreste de Talavera" and the Literature of Love*, Occasional Papers in Modern Languages, 7 (Hull: University of Hull, 1970), p. 60. See also Martín de Riquer, ed., *Arcipreste de Talavera*, p. 13; and Penna, pp. xlvii–li.

14. Whitbourn, pp. 59–60.

15. *Ibid.*, pp. 60–61.

16. Von Richthofen, p. 464, n. 1. Putting aside for the moment von Richthofen's proposal that there was possibly a manuscript tradition independent of the Contreras text (*ibid.*, p. 470), Miss Whitbourn comments that

> another circumstance which suggests that Martínez may not have been responsible for the *demanda* [epilogue] is that of its not appearing in the Escorial manuscript. This is the only extant version of the work dating from Martínez's lifetime, and therefore the only document in the preparation of which he could conceivably have been involved. If Martínez were the author of the epilogue and it was written before 1466, when Contreras finished his copy of the manuscript, it seems likely that it would have been included. It could, of course, have been written between 1466 and 1470, the probable date of Martínez's death, in which case the "año octavo" [eighth year] mentioned in the *demanda* would refer to 1468. Yet it seems extremely surprising that Martínez should have written it at this stage. The rest of the work had been completed thirty years before, and had been circulating in manuscript in the interim. Any stir it created, and any resentment to which it gave rise, must have passed into oblivion years before. Queen María, who is known to have been displeased, died in 1445. Why, more than twenty years later, should Martínez suddenly have decided to retract? (*The "Arcipreste de Talavera" and the Literature of Love*, pp. 61–62)

While this objection is well reasoned, if we suppose a much more accurate, now lost, manuscript tradition not reflected in the Contreras text, the "eighth year" mentioned in the epilogue could allude to 1438. As we know, Martínez finished the work on March 15, 1438, and thus may have emended it later that year. Immediately upon its completion, a copy of the *Archpriest of Talavera* must have begun to circulate freely at Juan II's court, and it is likely that if it did indeed anger the queen, it would have done so almost instantly after its publication. The Contreras codex, then, might well reflect an early draft of the Archpriest's work, while the text of the incunabula could stem from a subsequent revision of the original manuscript, including the epilogue, made sometime before 1439, but after March 15, 1438.

17. See Pedro Bach y Rita, *The Works of Perre Torroellas* (New York: Instituto de las Españas, 1930), pp. 192–215. For Tapia, see J. A. Balenchena, ed., *Cancionero general de Hernando del Castillo,* Sociedad de Bibliófilos Españoles, 21 (Madrid: Ginesta, 1882), II, 70, no. 856. Also of general interest concerning this point is Barbara Matulka, *The Novels of Juan Flores and Their European Diffusion* (New York: Institute of French Studies, 1931), pp. 116–19.

18. See Balenchena, I, no. 175.

19. Jacob Ornstein, "La misoginia y el profeminismo en la literatura castellana," *Revista de Filología Hispánica,* III (1941), 221–22. See also Matulka, p. 13.

20. Bach y Rita, pp. 70–71.

21. Francisco Icaza, ed., *El infamador, Los siete infantes de Lara, y el Ejemplar poético,* by Juan de la Cueva, Clásicos Castellanos, 60 (Madrid: La Lectura, 1924), pp. 99–100.

22. See Nicolás Antonio, *Biblioteca Hispana Vetus* (Matriti: Ioachimi Ibarrae, 1778), Liber X, Caput VI, vol. II, p. 249, no. 234. See also Antonio's *Biblioteca Hispana Nova* (Matriti: J. de Ibarra, 1783), I, 35.

23. Ludwig Lemcke, *Handbuch der spanischen Literatur* (Leipzig: Fleischer, 1855), I, 105–107.

24. Amador de los Ríos, VI, 277–85.

25. Marcelino Menéndez y Pelayo, *Orígenes de la novela* (Madrid: CSIC, 1943), I, 175–90.

26. Lesley Byrd Simpson, trans., *Little Sermons on Sin,* p. 6.

Chapter Three

1. Erich von Richthofen, "Alfonso Martínez de Toledo und sein *Arcipreste de Talauera,*" pp. 417–537.

2. Pedro Salinas, *Jorge Manrique, o tradición y originalidad,* 3rd ed. (Buenos Aires, Sudamericana, 1962), pp. 123–24.

3. Arturo Farinelli, "Note sulla Fortuna del *Corbaccio* nella Spagna Medievale," in *Bausteine zur romanischen Philologies Festgabe für Adolfo Mussafia* (Halle: Niemeyer, 1905), pp. 414–24. Boccaccio's *Corbaccio* is an elegantly contrived vindictive narrative

set in a typically late medieval allegorical framework similar to his *Amorosa Visione.* Whatever likeness exists between the Archpriest's ascetic tract and the Italian work is at best coincidental. Although the *Corbaccio,* like Martínez's work, is essentially didactic—written in order to combat lust and the excesses of courtly love—the structure, motif, and exposition of the two differ completely.

4. Farinelli (p. 419) points to a generically similar condemnation of cosmetics in *Il Corbaccio,* but the comparison of the texts is unconvincing.

5. Ludwig Lemcke, one of the earliest critics dealing with Martínez's work, insisted upon calling the *Archpriest of Talavera* the *Corbacho,* thus perpetuating in modern times its popular fifteenth-century title. See *Handbuch der spanischen Literatur* (Leipzig: F. Fleischer, 1855), I, 105. Théodore Joseph Boudet, Comte de Puymaigre, sees an etymological difference in the titles of the two works. He notes that "*Il Corbaccio* means the wicked crow, and *El Corbacho* signifies pizzle [a type of whip]. . . . This last title is easily explained in that the savage blows Alfonso Martínez rains down upon the fair sex evoke the flogging by a whip." *La Cour littéraire de don Juan II,* I, 156.

6. Von Richthofen, pp. 470–71. *The Fates of Illustrious Men* was translated into Castilian sometime before 1407 under the title *Caýda de príncipes* (*Fall of Princes*). See C. B. Bourland, "Boccaccio and the *Decameron* in Castilian and Catalan Literature," *Revue Hispanique,* XII (1905), 3.

7. Giovanni Boccaccio, *The Fates of Illustrious Men,* trans. Louis Brewer Hall (New York: F. Ungar, 1965), pp. 42–43. All subsequent citations are from this translation and noted within the text. For the original Latin, see Joannis Boccaci Certaldi, *De Casibus Virorum Illustrium,* ed. Louis Brewer Hall (1520; rpt. Gainesville, Florida: Scholars Facsimiles and Reprints, 1962), especially folios xi-xii.

8. See, for example, Geoffrey of Vinsauf, "Documentum de modo et arte dictandi et versificandi," II, 3 and 137–38, in Edmond Faral, *Les artes poétiques du XIIe siècle,* Bibliothèque de l'École des Hautes Études, 238 (Paris: Champion, 1924), p. 310.

9. J. González Muela, ed., *Arcipreste de Talavera,* by Alfonso Martínez de Toledo (Madrid: Castalia, 1970), p. 251. Hereafter cited in the text as *GM.*

10. See Mario Penna, ed., *Arcipreste de Talavera,* pp. xlii–xlvi.

11. Anna Krause, "Further Remarks on the Archpriest of Talavera," *Bulletin of Spanish Studies,* VI (1929), 59.

12. Von Richthofen, p. 451.

13. Andreas Capellanus, *The Art of Courtly Love,* trans. John J. Parry (New York: F. Ungar, 1959), p. 187. All subsequent references are given within the text. For the original Latin, see Andreae Capellani, *De Amore Libri Tres,* ed. Amadeu Pagès (Castellón de la Plana: Sociedad Castellonense de Cultura, 1930), especially pp. 181–209.

14. Von Richthofen, p. 452.

15. *Ibid.*, pp. 449–50.

16. Penna, p. 81.

17. Marcelino Menéndez y Pelayo recognizes this and notes that "the *Whip* is the only worthy antecedent capable of explaining the perfection of the prose in the *Celestina.*" *Orígenes de la novela,* I, 189–90.

18. María Rosa Lida de Malkiel, *La originalidad artística de "La Celestina,"* 2nd ed. (Buenos Aires: EUDEBA, 1970), pp. 81–107, but especially 91–92.

19. Dámaso Alonso, *De los siglos oscuros al de oro,* 2nd ed. (Madrid: Gredos, 1964), p. 126.

20. Von Richthofen, pp. 460–61.

21. We refer to Bartholomeus de Messana's Latin translation of the pseudo-Aristotelian *De Physiognomia.* See Richardus Foerster, *Scriptores Physiognomonici Graeci et Latini,* 2 vols. (Lipsiae: G. B. Teubneri, 1893).

22. See Jean Seznec, *The Survival of the Pagan Gods,* trans. Barbara Sessions (New York: Pantheon, 1953); and Walter Clyde Curry, "The Wife of Bath," in *Chaucer*, ed. Edward Wagenknecht (New York: Oxford-Galaxy, 1959), pp. 166–87.

23. See, for example, Vincent of Beauvais, *Speculum Maius*; Batholomeus Anglicus, *De Proprietatibus Rerum*; Roger Bacon, *Scriptum Principale*; Ioannes Baptista Porta, *Coelestis Physiognomoniae Libri Sex*; and Guido Bonatus, *Animae Astrologiae*. *The Secrets of Old Philosophers,* used by Martínez, is a translation (ca. 1135) of an Arabic text, *Sirr a'lasrar,* made by Johannes Hispalensis for Teresa, daughter of Alfonso VI of Castile. The work was very popular during the Middle Ages. There are two known vernacular versions that circulated in the Iberian Peninsula: a fifteenth-century Castilian verse translation (cf. *Poridat de las poridades*, ed. Lloyd Kasten [Madrid: S. Aguirre Torres, 1957]), and a fourteenth-century Aragonese version by Juan Fernández de Heredia. To determine whether Martínez used either of these, however, is probably impossible, because he only borrows the general theory of celestial physiognomy from the work. Moreover, since he refers to it by its Latin title, the

assumption that the *Whip* is dependent on one of the myriad Latin versions is probably the most correct.

Taking the word of the *Secreta Secretorum,* von Richthofen believes the theories of celestial physiognomy outlined in the *Whip* are from the Hippocratic tradition (*art. cit.,* 460–61). Rather than Hippocrates, however, it was Galen who declared that the stars played an active role in man's physical make-up. His treatise "That the Faculties of the Soul Follow the Temperaments of the Body" is heavily based upon astrological beliefs. Cf. David Riesman, *The Story of Medicine in the Middle Ages* (New York: Hoeber, 1936), pp. 98–106; and Owsei Temkin, *Galenism: Rise and Decline of a Medical Philosophy* (Ithaca: Cornell University Press, 1975).

24. For the English versions of this episode, see John Lydgate and Benedict Burgh's translation, *Secretes of Old Philisoffres,* ed. Robert Steele, Early English Text Society, ex. ser., 66 (London: Paul, Trench, Trübner, 1894), pp. 79–80; and *Three Prose Versions of the Secreta Secretorum,* ed. Robert Steele, Early English Text Society, ex. ser., 74 (London: Paul, 1898), pp. 38, 113, 217–18.

25. Von Richthofen, pp. 463–64.

26. See Petrus Paschasius, *Obras de San Pedro Pascual,* ed. Pedro Armengol Valenzuela, 4 vols. (Roma: Cuggiani, 1905–08), especially III, 54–91. For Aquinas on predestination, see his "Summa Contra Gentiles," III, caps. 82–93, in *Opera Omnia* (Romae: Riccardi Garroni, 1926), XIV, 243–87.

27. See Giuseppe Barbaglio, *Fede Acquisita e Fede Infusa secondo Duns Scoto, Occam e Biel* (Roma: Morcelliana, 1968), pp. 136–52, 223–27, 249–51.

28. See Robert Guelluy, *Philosophie et théologie chez Guillaume d'Ockham* (Louvain: Nauwelaerts, 1947), pp. 25–76.

29. See Étienne Gilson, *The Christian Philosophy of Saint Augustine,* trans. L. E. M. Lynch (New York: Random House, 1960), pp. 132–36.

30. Von Richthofen, pp. 462–64.

31. In fact, to make his use of quotations borrowed from Andreas more authoritative and veil his ignorance of their true origin, Martínez even spuriously attributes them to well-known authors. Andreas, for example, authorizes his thesis of woman's disobedience with the following unidentified reference to Ovid (*Amours,* III, iv, 17): "Therefore the remark of the wise man, 'We strive for what is forbidden, and always want what is denied us' " (*Art of Courtly Love,* p. 205). Not knowing to whom Capellanus refers, Martínez attributes the saying to Ptolemy (p. 133). Ptolemy was an ancient

revered by medieval writers, and thus mention of him lent weight to our author's use of the anonymous aphorism borrowed from the *Art of Courtly Love.*

32. See Von Richthofen, pp. 454, 463, 476; he attributes the *Compendium of Theological Truth* to Albertus Magnus (p. 454), and hence posits his influence upon Martínez de Toledo. The *Compendium*, however, was most likely written by Hugh of Strasburg. See Luzian Pfelger, "Der Dominikaner Hugo von Strassburg und das *Compendium Theologicae Veritatis*," *Zeitschrift für katolische Theologie*, XXVIII (1904), 429–40; also, Joseph Schroeder, "Hugh of Strasburg," *Catholic Encyclopedia* (New York: Appleton, 1910), VII, 523–24. Moreover, the allusions to *Gratian's Decree* in the *Whip* do not necessarily reflect a direct quotation from it. *Gratian's Decree* is the basis of the *Body of Canon Law,* a work Martínez did know directly. His references to the *Decree* are probably through this work.

33. Menéndez y Pelayo, *Orígenes de la novela,* I, 176.

34. *Ibid.*

35. Juan Ruiz, *Libro de buen amor,* ed. J. Cejador y Frauca, Clásicos Castellanos, 14 (Madrid: Espasa-Calpe, 1963), I, 81. All subsequent citations are from this edition and noted by stanza number within the text.

36. Martín de Riquer, ed., *Arcipreste de Talavera,* p. 226, n. 1.

37. See Otis H. Green, "On Juan Ruiz's Parody of the Canonical Hours," *Hispanic Review,* XXVI (1958), 12–34. In stanza 389, Ruiz alludes to a religion of love and calls those who follow it heretics.

38. See Dorothy Clotelle Clarke, "Juan Ruiz and Andreas Capellanus," *Hispanic Review,* XL (1972), 390–411. Also, Brian Dutton, "*Buen amor*: Its Meaning and Uses," in *Libro de buen amor Studies,* ed. G. B. Gybbon-Monnypenny (London: Tamesis, 1970), pp. 95–121.

39. See Peter Dunn, "De las figuras del arcipreste," in Gybbon-Monnypenny, pp. 79–93. Also, Walter Clyde Curry; and María Rosa Lida, "Notas sobre el *Libro de buen amor,*" *Revista de Filología Hispánica,* III (1940), 122–25.

40. See Ramón Menéndez Pidal, "Notas al libro del arcipreste de Hita," in his *Poesía árabe y poesía europea,* Colección Austral, 190 (Madrid: Espasa-Calpe, 1963), pp. 139–57.

41. Von Richthofen, p. 428.

42. Anecdotes based on personal reminiscence are a favorite strategy of medieval preachers. See G. R. Owst, *Preaching in Medieval England* (Cambridge: The University Press, 1926), pp. 60–64.

43. Von Richthofen, pp. 465–96.

44. Kenneth Jackson, *The International Popular Tale and Early Welsh Tradition* (Cardiff: University of Wales Press, 1961), p. 49.

45. Juan Manuel, *El Conde Lucanor,* ed. E. Juliá (Madrid: Victoriano Suárez, 1933), p. 157.

46. Menéndez y Pelayo, for example, falls prey to the assumption that Juan de Ausim was probably an error for Jean Gerson (*Orígenes de la novela,* I, 181, n. 3).

47. See his *Historia crítica de la literatura española,* VI, 282, n. 1. Also, C. J. Whitbourn, *The "Arcipreste de Talavera" and the Literature of Love,* pp. 25–27. We know Martínez once owned a copy of the *Book of the Ladies,* but the date of purchase written in the *ex libris* is ten years after the *Whip* was completed.

48. In a contrived effort, too complex and long to repeat here, he attempts to explain how paleographically *Juan de Ausim* is probably a reference to Andreas Capellanus. See Mario Penna, pp. xviii–xix.

49. Review of *Arcipreste de Talavera,* ed. Mario Penna, in *Speculum,* XXXI (1956), 397–98.

50. Raúl A. del Piero, "El Arcipreste de Talavera y Juan de Ausim," *Bulletin Hispanique,* LXII (1960), 125–35.

51. See, for example, Pero López de Ayala's *Flores de los morales de Job,* ed. F. Branciforti (Firenze: Le Monnier, 1963). We have already noted that the *Morals on the Book of Job* is cited and mentioned throughout the *Compendium of Theological Truth.*

Chapter Four

1. Juan Beneyto, "Teoría cuatrocentista de la oratoria," *Boletín de la Real Academia Española,* XXIV (1945), 420.

2. Erich von Richthofen, "Alfonso Martínez de Toledo und sein *Arcipreste de Talauera,*" p. 503.

3. Marcelino Menéndez y Pelayo, *Orígenes de la novela,* I, 181.

4. "Tractatulus Eximii Doctoris Henrici de Hassia de Arte Praedicandi Valde Utilis," in Harry Caplan, *Of Eloquence,* ed. Anne King and Helen North (Ithaca: Cornell University Press, 1970), p. 147. For a full description of the medieval sermon, see our "*Ars Praedicandi* and the Structure of *Arcipreste de Talavera,* Part I," *Hispania,* LVIII (1975), 430–32.

5. Otto Dieter, "*Arbor Picta*: The Medieval Tree of Preaching," *Quarterly Journal of Speech,* LI (1965), 131. It is significant that *El espéculo de los legos,* a preaching manual, concerns itself with the love of God as a theme for sermons. See José M. Mohedano

Hernández, ed., *El espéculo de los legos* (Madrid: CSIC, 1951), pp. 20–23.

6. A. Lecoy de la Marche, *La Chaire française au moyen age*, 2nd ed. (Paris: Renouard, 1886), p. 292.

7. The missing protheme and short "generalizing reflections on the theme of the homily" constitute a subgenre of sermon according to Lecoy de la Marche, pp. 291–92.

8. Von Richthofen, pp. 507–508.

9. María Rosa Lida de Malkiel studies don Juan Manuel's literary relationship to medieval preaching in her "Tres notas sobre don Juan Manuel," in *Estudios de literatura española y comparada* (Buenos Aires: EUDEBA, 1966), pp. 92–133.

10. Edwin Dargan, *A History of Preaching* (London: Hodder and Stoughton, 1905), I, 305–306. Robert of Basevorn declares that "I have not seen it mentioned in any authentic author [of *artes praedicandi*] that such a prayer ought to be said before the theme, yet I have frequently seen it done. It is proper, whether before or immediately after the theme, because both theme and prayer should be said in the beginning"; in Th.-M. Charland, *Artes Praedicandi*, Publications de l'Institut d'Études Médiévales d'Ottawa, 7 (Ottawa: Institut d'Études Médiévales, 1936), p. 263.

11. In Caplan, p. 155.

12. Charland, p. 329.

13. Lecoy de la Marche (pp. 206–207) notes that the sermon would vary according to the audience for whom it was intended. Many medieval sermons exhibit both popular and learned tendencies. See Homer C. Pfander, *The Popular Sermon of the Medieval Friar in England* (New York: New York University Press, 1932), pp. 26–29.

14. Caplan notes that an alternative to dividing the theme was to show its relevancy to daily life. Essentially, this is the procedure followed by Martínez. The marking of opposites "should [also] be used in every sermon in order that evil deeds committed may not be deemed likely to prove other than evil" (pp. 62–67).

15. The analogy of the sermon to musical composition is not alien to the Spanish pulpit. See Francisco Terrones del Caño, *Instrucción de predicadores*, Clásicos Castellanos, 126 (Madrid: Espasa-Calpe, 1960), p. 104.

16. See Lecoy de la Marche, p. 311; and also G. R. Owst, *Literature and Pulpit in Medieval England*, 2nd ed. (Oxford: Basil Blackwell, 1966), pp. 507–11, 541–42.

17. Mohedano Hernández, pp. 248–55. In fact, several chapters in the first part of the *Whip* bear a striking resemblance to the

Mirror. For example, Chapter XVII, "How the learned lose their learning through love," uses arguments very similar to those in Chapter VII, "Concerning carnal love," of the preaching manual.

18. In his study of Hortensio de Paravicino's orations, Emilio Alarcos confirms the basic structure of the sermon: "In a zig-zag, rambling manner, the orator proves and develops his thesis, relating it directly, or indirectly through the medium of exempla, to the diverse circumstances of the sermon and its consequent moral application." "Los sermones de Paravicino," *Revista de Filología Española,* XXIV (1937), 268.

19. Terrones del Caño (p. 117) describes a similar process.

20. Commenting on Chapters XIX–XXXVIII of the *Whip*, Mario Penna observes that "the disposition and organization of the material recall those we find in the exempla handbooks used by medieval preachers. It is therefore possible that the Archpriest had one at hand in order to systematize his exposition. He must certainly have been familiar with these manuals." Mario Penna, ed., *Arcipreste de Talavera,* p. xxix.

21. The original Spanish of this passage is better translated as follows: "further, that love is the cause of committing the seven deadly sins, for there is not a single one which is not committed by lovers as you will see by following our process." The *process* mentioned here is doubtless the technical process of sermonic exegesis.

22. Describing this technique, Terrones del Caño admonishes that "the first considerations should contain more and be longer, since there is still patience to hear them. The other ones, the closer they are to the end, should be shorter so as not to try the audience. Frequent change near the end abates boredom" (p. 114).

23. Caplan, p. 78.

24. For the textual problems of the *Whip,* see von Richthofen, pp. 437–44; Penna, pp. xxxiii–li.

25. Lecoy de la Marche, p. 296.

26. In Roque Chabás, "Estudio sobre los sermones valencianos de San Vicente Ferrer," *Revista de Archivos, Bibliotecas y Museos,* VI (1902), 155. Since Chabás's study appears serialized in three consecutive volumes of the *Revista de Archivos, Bibliotecas y Museos,* and since we shall frequently refer to it, all references will be given within the text showing the volume and page number of the journal preceded by the name Chabás.

27. Von Richthofen, pp. 501–502.

28. See Chabás, IX (1903), p. 88; and Pfander, p. 6.

29. Pfander, p. 6.

30. See J. Rodríguez-Puértolas, *Fray Iñigo de Mendoza y sus "Coplas de Vita Christi"* (Madrid: Gredos, 1968), pp. 148–65 and 172–74.

31. Erich Auerbach, *Mimesis, the Representation of Reality in Western Literature*, trans. W. R. Trask (Princeton: Princeton University Press, 1968), p. 162.

32. Von Richthofen, pp. 507–508.

33. Françesc Eiximenis, "Ars Praedicandi," ed P. Martí de Barcelona, in *Homenatge a Antoni Rubió i Lluch* (Barcelona: n.p., 1936), II, 310.

34. In Caplan, p. 156.

35. Compare, for example, J. González Muela, ed., *Arcipreste de Talavera*, p. 88, 124–25, 129, 168, 169, 141, 121, and Chabás, VII (1902), 140–41, 133, 422; IX (1903), 90.

36. Martín de Córdoba, "Ars Praedicandi," ed. Fernando Rubio, in *Ciudad de Dios*, CLXXII (1959), 330.

37. *Ibid.*, p. 336.

38. See Saint Augustine, *First Catechetical Instruction*, trans. J. P. Christopher (Westminster, Md.: Newman Press, 1962), pp. 43, and 116, n. 125.

39. Lecoy de la Marche, p. 216.

40. In Martí de Riquer, *Història de la literatura catalana* (Barcelona: Ariel, 1964), II, 239.

41. Von Richthofen, p. 504.

42. J. Th. Welter, *L'Exemplum dans la Littérature Religieuse et Didactique du Moyen Age* (Paris: Guitard, 1927), pp. 80–81. To this day, formulism plays an important part in sermon development. See the following by Bruce A. Rosenberg: "The Oral Quality of Reverend Shegog's Sermon in Faulkner's *The Sound and the Fury*," *Literatur in Wissenschaft und Unterricht*, II (1969), 73–88; *The Art of the American Folk Preacher* (New York: Oxford, 1970); "The Formulaic Quality of Spontaneous Sermons," *Journal of American Folklore*, LXXXIII (1970), 3–20; "The Genre of the Folk Sermon," *Genre*, IV (1971), 189–211. We owe these references to the kindness of our friend and teacher, Professor Samuel G. Armistead.

43. Dámaso Alonso, *De los siglos oscuros al de oro*, p. 135.

44. Caplan, p. 89.

45. Caplan (p. 71) translates a late medieval preaching tract counseling the use of *adnominatio*. See also Janet Chapman, "Juan Ruiz's Learned Sermon," in *Libro de buen amor Studies* (London: Tamesis, 1970), pp. 43–44.

46. Alonso, p. 135.

47. See, for example, Charland, p. 335.
48. Von Richthofen, p. 520. For Pérez Pastor's comments, see C. Pérez Pastor, ed., *Arcipreste de Talavera*, p. vi.
49. See *De Doctrina Christiana*, Book IV, Chapter 20; also Henri I. Marrou, *Saint Augustine et la Fin de la Culture Antique* (Paris: E. de Boccard, 1938), pp. 80–81.
50. Pfander, p. 45.
51. See von Richthofen, p. 520.
52. Menéndez y Pelayo, *Orígenes de la novela*, I, 189. The dialogues and monologues of the *Whip* lead Angel del Río to believe it is "clearly the precursor of the realist novel." *Historia de la literatura española*, rev. ed. (New York: Holt, Rinehart and Winston, 1966), I, 147.
53. Bourgain, *La Chaire française au XIIe siècle* (Paris: Librairie Catholique, 1879), p. 211.
54. *Ibid.*, p. 214.
55. Christine J. Whitbourn traces the reprobation of lust in the preaching tradition up to the Archpriest's work. See her *"Arcipreste de Talavera" and the Literature of Love.*
56. Cited in *The Legacy of the Middle Ages*, ed. C. G. Crump (Oxford: Oxford, 1938), p. 403. For the literary view of women in the Middle Ages, see Alice Adèle Hentsch, *De la Littérature didactique du moyen age s'adressant spécialement aux femmes* (Cambridge, England: A. Coueslant, 1903).
57. Owst, p. 390.
58. Whitbourn (pp. 37, 43, 47–52) and von Richthofen (pp. 496–97) tend to understate Martínez's antifeminism by arguing that he treats men equally harshly. While this is his stated intent, he nevertheless accords the preponderance of his criticism to women. It is, we believe, also significant that the *Archpriest of Talavera* was viewed as antifeminist by its early reading public: doña María saw it as a misogynistic work, as did Juan Justiniano, Juan de la Cueva, and, obviously, the author of the epilogue. Even the early iconography of the work judged it antifeminist. The woodcut of the 1547 edition (Seville: Andrés de Burgos) clearly portrays the Archpriest arguing heatedly with a woman. Despite Martínez's own qualifications, the *Whip* throughout the centuries has impressed the majority of its public as misogynistic. As Katharine Rogers notes in her study of misogyny in literature:

> Sometimes the [antifeminist] author is more concerned with satirizing a vice found in women than women themselves, or with being funny than satirizing at all. Sometimes he dissociates

the misogynistic sentiments from his point of view. Sometimes his criticism is so lightly hostile that it is compatible with general respect and liking for women. These modifying factors must of course be taken into account in interpreting antifeminist statements found in literary works. But they do not cause the antifeminism to evaporate. . . . Since most writers have not felt free to express misogyny directly—it is an unnatural attitude, considered shocking in most periods—they have found it necessary to conceal it in some way, both from others and from themselves. Misogyny, therefore, is more apt than not to appear in a disguised form." (*The Troublesome Helpmate, a History of Misogyny in Literature* [Seattle: University of Washington Press, 1966], pp. xi–xii)

A glance at the chapter headings in Part II of the *Whip* and a comparison with their counterparts in Part III is sufficient to confirm Martínez's antifeminism.

59. Lecoy de la Marche, p. 438.

60. Owst, p. 393.

61. See *ibid.*, p. 118.

62. Lesley Byrd Simpson, trans., *Little Sermons on Sin*, p. 3.

63. Mohedano Hernández, p. 249.

64. Owst, p. 381.

65. Lecoy de la Marche, p. 428.

66. Owst, p. 232. Johan Huizinga notes that "since the thirteenth century, the popular preaching of the mendicant orders had made the eternal admonition to remember death swell into a sombre chorus ringing throughout the world" (*The Waning of the Middle Ages* (New York: Anchor, 1954), p. 138. See also Norman Cohn, *The Pursuit of the Millenium* (New York: Oxford, 1970), especially pp. 148–86.

67. Lecoy de la Marche, p. 354.

68. See Owst, pp. 243–45; and Lecoy de la Marche, pp. 348–66.

69. Menéndez y Pelayo, *Orígenes de la novela,* I, 181.

70. Miguel Herrero García, "Nueva interpretación de la novela picaresca," *Revista de Filología Española,* XXIV (1937), 350.

71. See Marcelino Menéndez y Pelayo, *Historia de los heterodoxos españoles,* ed. A. Bonilla y San Martín (Madrid: V. Suárez, 1917), III, 231–33.

72. The Beghards pursued a quietist devotion like the later *alumbrados* ("enlightened ones"). Significantly, Eugenio Asensio offers the following words: "The first time the word *aluminado*—a semi-Italian derivative phonetically related to *alumbrado*—appears in a

Castilian text it is applied purely and simply to homosexuals." Asensio then cites the text in F. López de Villalobos's *Sumario de la medicina* (*The Summary of Medicine*), Burgos, 1498. See "El erasmismo y las corrientes espirituales afines," *Revista de Filología Española,* XXXVI (1952), 71.

73. Keith Whinnom, "El origen de las comparaciones religiosas del Siglo de Oro: Mendoza, Montesino, y Román," *Revista de Filología Española,* XLVI (1963), 280–81.

74. Owst, pp. 51–52.

75. Lecoy de la Marche, p. 342.

76. See Owst, pp. 54–55.

77. Instruction, entertainment, and persuasion are considered fundamental to the art of preaching by Saint Augustine. See his *De Doctrina Christiana,* Book IV, Chapter 26.

78. In another of his works, a translation of San Ildefonso's *De Virginitate Sanctae Mariae Contra Tres Infideles,* Martínez clearly anticipates what in the latter part of the fifteenth century was to become a great point of contention between Castilian Franciscans and Dominicans. His defense of the Immaculate Conception aligns him intellectually with the former. See José Madoz y Moleres, ed., *San Ildefonso de Toledo a través de la pluma del arcipreste de Talavera,* by Alfonso Martínez de Toledo, Biblioteca de Antiguos Escritores Españoles, 2 (Madrid:CSIC, 1943), pp. 103–81; and Alejandro Recio, "La Inmaculada Concepción en la predicación franciscano-española," *Archivo Ibero-Americano,* XV (1955), 105–200.

Chapter Five

1. For an excellent summary of the polemic, see June Hall Martin, *Love's Fools: Aucassin, Troilus, Calisto and the Parody of the Courtly Lover* (London: Tamesis, 1972), pp. 1–21.

2. See E. Talbot Donaldson, "The Myth of Courtly Love," in his *Speaking of Chaucer* (London: Athlone, 1970), pp. 154–63; and Peter Dronke, *Medieval Latin and the Rise of the European Love Lyric* (Oxford: The University Press, 1965), I, 1–56.

3. Dronke, p. 2.

4. A. J. Denomy, *The Heresy of Courtly Love* (New York: D. X. McMullen, 1947), p. 20.

5. Cited by Otis H. Green, "Courtly Love in the Spanish *Cancioneros,*" in his *Literary Mind of Medieval and Renaissance Spain* (Lexington: University of Kentucky Press, 1970), p. 49.

6. *Ibid.,* pp. 49–50.

7. *Ibid.,* p. 50.

8. William George Dodd, *Courtly Love in Gower and Chaucer* (Gloucester, Mass.: Peter Smith, 1959), p. 10. A complete study of the courtly lady's ideal beauty may be found in Alice M. Colby, *The Portrait in Twelfth-Century French Literature: An Example of the Stylistic Originality of Chrétien de Troyes* (Geneva: Droz, 1965), pp. 25–72.

9. A. J. Denomy, "*Fin' Amors*: The Pure Love of the Troubadours, Its Amorality and Possible Sources," *Medieval Studies*, VII (1945), 142.

10. See Gaston Paris, "Lancelot du Lac: Le Conte de la Charette," *Romania*, XII (1883), 518; Moshé Lazar, *Amour courtois et "Fin' Amors" dans la littérature du XIIe siècle* (Paris: C. Klincksieck, 1964), p. 136; and Otis Green, pp. 65–74.

11. Martin, p. 8.

12. In his "Cadira del honor," in *Obras de Juan Rodríguez de la Cámara ó del Padrón*, ed. A. Paz y Melia, Sociedad de Bibliófilos Españoles, 22 (Madrid: M. Ginesta, 1884), p. 137.

13. See Green, especially p. 67.

14. Quoted in Diego Catalán de Menéndez Pidal, "Ideales moriscos en una crónica de 1344," *Nueva Revista de Filología Hispánica*, VII (1954), 574.

15. See *Poetas castellanos anteriores al siglo XV*, ed. Tomás Antonio Sánchez, Biblioteca de Autores Españoles, 57 (Madrid: Rivadeneyra, 1864), p. 489, stanza 387.

16. See Pero Rodríguez de Lena, *El passo honroso* (Madrid: A. de Sancha, 1783). Quiñones was reputed to have worn a heavy chain around his neck on Thursdays, symbolizing his enslavement to the wishes of his lady. For similar fifteenth-century courtly and chivalric exploits, see Martín de Riquer, *Caballeros andantes españoles*, Colección Austral, 1397 (Madrid: Espasa-Calpe, 1967); also J. Huizinga, *The Waning of the Middle Ages* (New York: Anchor, 1954), pp. 67–138.

17. See C. S. Lewis, *The Allegory of Love* (London: Oxford University Press, 1953), pp. 18, 20–21, 29–32.

18. By Juan Rodríguez del Padrón. See J. A. Balenchena, ed., *Cancionero General de Hernando del Castillo*, Sociedad de Bibliófilos Españoles, 20–21 (Madrid: Ginesta, 1882), I, 371 ff.

19. By Suero de Ribera. See R. Foulché-Delbosc, ed., *Cancionero Castellano del siglo XV* (Madrid: Bailly-Bailliere, 1912), I, 190.

20. For example, Diego de San Pedro. See his *Obras completas*, ed. Keith Whinnom (Madrid: Castalia, 1973), I, 172–83.

21. By Garci Sánchez de Badajoz. See Francisca Vendrell de Millás, ed., *El Cancionero de Palacio* (Barcelona: CSIC, 1945), p. 13.

22. See, for example, the ones composed by Juan Agraz and Garci Sánchez de Badajoz in Foulché-Delbosc, II, 209 and 625.

23. See Green, pp. 45–46.

24. The Marqués de Santillana's Sonnet 14 compares the sight of his lady to the vision of Christ's transfiguration on Mount Tabor. See his *Obras*, ed. J. Amador de los Ríos (Madrid: Rodríguez, 1852), p. 281.

25. See Green, p. 69.

26. Kenelm Foster, *Courtly Love and Christianity*, Aquinas Socity of London, Aquinas Paper, 39 (London: Aquin Press, 1963), p. 22.

27. Keith Whinnom believes the poetic casuistry of the *cancionero* ("songbook") poets, especially those from Juan II's time, is fraught with obscenities and sublimated eroticism. See his "Hacia una interpretación y apreciación de la canciones del *Cancionero General*," *Filología*, XII (1968–69), 361–81. A. J. Foreman arrives at similar conclusions in "The Cancionero Poet Quirós" (M.A. Thesis, Westfield College, London, 1969).

28. Christine J. Whitbourn, *The "Arcipreste de Talavera" and the Literature of Love*, p. 35.

29. *Ibid.*, pp. 43–44.

30. Giovanni Boccaccio, *The Fates of Illustrious Men*, trans. Louis Brewer Hall (New York: F. Ungar, 1965), pp. 117–18.

31. See Maurice Valency, *In Praise of Love: An Introduction to the Love Poetry of the Renaissance* (New York: Macmillan, 1958), pp. 2–3.

32. See, for example, the *Summa Theologica* of Saint Thomas Aquinas (2-2, q. 150, a. 1; 2-2, q. 151, a. 2; 2-2, q. 154, a. 8). It was probably for this reason Capellanus's *Art of Courtly Love* was condemned by Bishop Tempier in 1277; see A. J. Denomy, "The *De Amore* of Andreas Capellanus and the Condemnation of 1277," *Medieval Studies*, XV (1953), 107–49.

33. Whitbourn, p. 48.

34. *Ibid.*, p. 36.

35. Green, pp. 82–83.

36. Lesley Byrd Simpson, trans., *Little Sermons on Sin*, p. 8.

37. Indeed, the romantic lover's belief in predestination seems to be a favorite target of those wishing to discredit the idealized tradition. Troilus's long speech on the subject in book four of Chaucer's *Troilus and Criseyde*, for example, is designed to underline the heterodoxy of courtly love.

38. See Whitbourn, pp. 53–54.

39. See Andreae Capellani, *De Amore Libri Tres*, ed. Amadeu Pagès (Castellón de la Plana: Sociedad Castellonense de Cultura, 1930), pp. ix–xvi. On the one hand, the title *Rules of Love* confirms that Book III was not translated, while on the other it buttresses the opinion that there was in fact a *code* of love.

40. Erich von Richthofen feels that Martínez was probably not familiar with Books I and II of Andreas's work because he alludes to neither of them in the *Whip* (Von Richthofen, "Alfonso Martínez de Toledo und sein *Arcipreste de Talavera*," p. 453). Nevertheless, if Martínez's purpose was to indict courtly love, he would naturally avoid referring to Books I and II.

Chapter Six

1. See Jacob Ornstein, "La misoginia y el profeminismo en la literatura castellana," p. 222; also María del Pilar Oñate, *El feminismo en la literatura española* (Madrid: Espasa-Calpe, 1938), pp. 39–40.

2. The mid-thirteenth-century translation of the Oriental *Sindibad*, the *Libro de los engaños* (*Book of Deceits*), is a notably antifeminist work. Nevertheless, it should be looked at as an early and, therefore, isolated case of Castilian misogyny. See *El libro de los engaños*, ed. J. E. Keller (Chapel Hill: University of North Carolina Press, 1959).

3. *Obras de Juan Rodríguez de la Cámara ó del Padrón*, ed. A. Paz y Melia (Madrid: Ginesta, 1884), p. 87.

4. *Tratado de las epístolas de Mosén Diego de Valera*, ed. J. A. de Balenchena, Sociedad de Bibliófilos Españoles, 16 (Madrid: Ginesta, 1878), p. 127. The allusion to a "new sect" of maligners is significant. It implies that misogyny was a relatively new phenomenon in Castile.

5. Alvaro de Luna, *Libro de las virtuosas e claras mugeres,* ed. Manuel Castillo, 2nd ed. (Valencia: Prometeo, 1917), p. 17.

6. Ornstein, p. 222.

7. See *Obras de Diego de San Pedro*, ed. Keith Whinnom (Madrid: Castalia, 1973), I, 64–69. Whinnom also composed a volume on San Pedro for the Twayne World Authors Series (New York: Twayne, 1974).

8. *Obras de Diego de San Pedro*, ed. Keith Whinnom, I, 173.

9. Luis de Lucena, *Repetición de amores*, ed. Jacob Ornstein (Chapel Hill: University of North Carolina Press, 1954), p. 74.

10. *Ibid.*, p. 82.

11. Erich von Richthofen, "Alfonso Martínez de Toledo und sein *Arcipreste de Talauera*," pp. 487–88.

12. *Rodrigo de Reinosa*, ed. J. M. de Cossío, Antología de Escritores Montañeses, 16 (Santander: Librería Moderna, 1950), pp. 30–32, 36.

13. Von Richthofen, p. 526.

14. See G. D. Trotter, "The *Coplas de las comadres* of Rodrigo de Reinosa and *La Celestina*," in *Studia Philologica, Homenaje a Dámaso Alonso* (Madrid: Gredos, 1960), III, 527–37; also, Stephen Gilman and Michael Ruggerio, "Rodrigo de Reinosa and *La Celestina*," *Romanische Forschungen*, LXXIII (1961), 255–84.

15. See his "*El Corbacho*: las interpolaciones y la deuda de *La Celestina*," *Homenaje a Antonio Rodríguez-Moñino* (Madrid: Castalia, 1966), II, 115–20.

16. See the following: Ferdinand Wolf, *Studien zur Geschichte der spanischen und portugiesischen Nationalliteratur* (Berlin: Asher, 1859), p. 235; Marcelino Menéndez y Pelayo, *Orígenes de la novela*, I, 181; III, 346–49; Fernando de Rojas, *La Celestina*, ed. J. Cejador y Frauca, Clásicos Castellanos, 20, 23 (Madrid: Espasa-Calpe, 1968), I, xx, 48 n. 4, 50 n. 8; 52 n. 7, 57 n. 14, 58 n. 19, 72 n. 1, 107 n. 9; Florentino Castro Guisasola, *Observaciones sobre las fuentes literarias de "La Celestina,"* supplement of the *Revista de Filología Española*, 5 (Madrid: Jiménez y Molina, 1924), 175–76; María Rosa Lida de Malkiel, *La originalidad artística de "La Celestina,"* 2nd ed. (Buenos Aires: EUDEBA, 1970), pp. 112–13, 179, 223, 231, 252, 322, 334–37, 425, 429, 480, 489, 499, 510, 526–27, 565–66, 630, 644, 673, 676, 682–84, 708–709.

17. Fernando de Rojas, *La Celestina*, I, 27.

18. For this aspect of *La Celestina* see Otis H. Green, "La furia de Melibea," *Clavileño* (1953), 1–3; J. M. Aguirre, *Calisto y Melibea, amantes cortesanos* (Zaragoza: Almenara, 1962); E. J. Webber, "The *Celestina* as an *Arte de Amores*," *Modern Philology*, LV (1958), 145–53.

19. See Théodore Joseph Boudet, Comte de Puymaigre, *La Cour littéraire de don Juan II*, I, 166.

20. Dorothy Clotelle Clarke, *Allegory, Decalogue, and Deadly Sins in "La Celestina,"* University of California Publications in Modern Philology, 91 (Berkeley: University of California Press, 1968), pp. 43–44.

21. Menéndez y Pelayo, *Orígenes de la novela*, III, 346.

22. Stephen Gilman, *The Art of "La Celestina"* (Madison: University of Wisconsin Press, 1956), pp. 29–30. Ramón Menéndez

Pidal also feels that Martínez's dialogues lack sophistication and that "they are no more developed than those we find in [Juan Manuel's] *Lucanor.*" See his *Antología de prosistas españoles*, Colección Austral, 110 (Madrid: Espasa-Calpe, 1964), p. 44.

23. Carmelo Samonà, *Aspetti del Retoricismo nella "Celestina,"* Studi di Letteratura Spagnola, Facoltà di Magisterio dell' Università di Roma, 2 (Roma: Tipografia Agostiniana, 1953), p. 224.

24. *Ibid.*, p. 136. For the complete textual and stylistic parallels, see our "*Celestina*, Act I: Cota, Mena . . . or Alfonso Martínez de Toledo?" forthcoming in *Kentucky Romance Quarterly*, 1976.

25. See F. Landmann, "Shakespeare and Euphuism," *New Shakespeare Society Transactions*, series 1, IX (1880–85), 241–76.

26. Francisco Márquez Villanueva, *Espiritualidad y literatura en el siglo XVI* (Madrid: Alfaguara, 1968), p. 43.

27. Von Richthofen, "Alfonso Martínez de Toledo und sein Arcipreste," p. 534.

28. See Fray Antonio de Guevara, *Menosprecio de corte y alabanza de aldea*, ed. M. Martínez de Burgos, Clásicos Castellanos, 29 (Madrid: Espasa-Calpe, 1967), p. xix.

29. *Ibid.*, p. 123.

30. María Rosa Lida, "Fray Antonio de Guevara, Edad Media y Siglo de Oro español," *Revista de Filología Hispánica*, VII (1945), 359.

31. Cited in Márquez Villanueva, pp. 41–42.

32. *Ibid.*, p. 45.

33. Guevara, pp. 121–22.

34. Márquez Villanueva (pp. 47–56) points out Guevara's debt to the pulpit.

35. See Bruno Damiani, *Francisco Delicado*, TWAS, 335 (New York: Twayne, 1974).

36. *Ibid.*, p. 32.

37. Francisco Delicado, *La lozana andaluza*, ed. Joaquín del Val (Madrid: Taurus, 1967), p. 209.

38. Menéndez y Pelayo, *Orígenes de la novela*, I, 190.

39. Helmut Hatzfeld, *Don Quijote como obra de arte del lenguaje*, trans. M. C. de I (Madrid: CSIC, 1949), pp. 11, 111.

40. *Ibid.*, p. 228.

41. See *ibid.*, pp. 291 and 329–30.

42. See Américo Castro, *El pensamiento de Cervantes*, 2nd ed. (Barcelona: Noguer, 1972), pp. 182–91.

43. *Ibid.*

44. For these proverbs in *Don Quijote* see Miguel de Cervantes

Saavedra, *El ingenioso hidalgo don Quijote de la Mancha,* ed. J. García Soriano *et al.*, 10th ed. (Madrid: Aguilar, 1965), pp. 1295, 903, 1374, respectively. The Archpriest's citations of the same proverbs may be found in Mario Penna, ed., *Arcipreste de Talavera,* pp. 149, 101, 44, respectively.

45. Von Richthofen, "Alfonso Martínez und sein *Arcipreste*," p. 532.

Chapter Seven

1. José Madoz y Moleres, ed., *San Ildefonso de Toledo a través de la pluma del Arcipreste de Talavera,* by Alfonso Martínez de Toledo (Madrid: CSIC, 1943), p. 40.
2. See Enrique Flórez, *España Sagrada* (Madrid: M. F. Rodríguez, 1918), V, 344 and 501–25.
3. See *Poetas castellanos anteriores al siglo XV*, ed. Tomás Antonio Sánchez, Biblioteca de Autores Españoles, 57 (Madrid: Rivadeneyra, 1864), pp. 323–30.
4. Madoz y Moleres, p. 19.
5. *Ibid.*, p. 21.
6. Madoz y Moleres publishes Martínez's translation in its entirety in *San Ildefonso de Toledo*, pp. 103–81.
7. See *ibid.*, pp. 29–30.
8. *Ibid.*, pp. 25–27.
9. See her "Fray Antonio de Guevara," *Revista de Filología Hispánica,* VII (1945), 379–84; and also her "Perduración de la literatura antigua en Occidente," *Romance Philology,* V (1951–52), 99–131; as well as her "Las sectas judías y los 'procuradores' romanos: En torno a Josefo y su influjo sobre la literatura española," *Hispanic Review,* XXXIX (1971), 183–219. Also of interest is José Amador de los Ríos, *Historia crítica de la literatura española,* I, 416–17; II, 48–49, 58, 65, 101–102, 142–43, 155–56, 182, 316–18; VI, 246.
10. See, for example, Erasmo Buceta, "La tendencia de identificar el español con el latín: Un episodio cuatrocentista," *Homenaje a Menéndez Pidal* (Madrid: Hernando, 1925), I, 85–108.
11. Madoz y Moleres, pp. lxxxvii–xciv.
12. Diego de Colmenares, *Historia de Segovia* (Madrid: Diego Laínez, 1640), p. 63.
13. Raúl A. del Piero, "La tradición textual de *La atalaya de las corónicas* del Arcipreste de Talavera," *Publications of the Modern Language Association,* LXXXI (1966), 12–22.
14. See Raúl del Piero, "*La corónica de Mahomad* del Arcipreste de Talavera," *Nueva Revista de Filología Hispánica*, XIV (1960), 21–50.

15. In Raúl del Piero, *Dos escritores de la baja Edad Media castellana (Pedro de Veragüe y el Arcipreste de Talavera, cronista real)*, supplement of the *Boletín de la Real Academia Española*, 23 (Madrid: Aguirre, 1971), p. 116.

16. *Ibid.*, pp. 90–98.

17. According to del Piero, Martínez likely used manuscript *U* of the *Primera Crónica General*. See *Dos escritores*, p. 98, n. 26.

18. James Fitzmaurice-Kelly, *A New History of Spanish Literature* (Oxford: Oxford University Press, 1926), p. 107; Benito Sánchez Alonso, *Historia de la historiografía española* (Madrid: CSIC, 1947), II, 317.

19. Del Piero, *Dos escritores*, pp. 95–96.

20. Georges Cirot, "Note sur l'*Atalaya* de l'Archiprêtre de Talavera," in *Homenaje a Menéndez Pidal* (Madrid: Hernando, 1925), I, 355–69; also his "Notes Complémentaires sur l'*Atalaya* de l'Archiprêtre de Talavera," *Bulletin Hispanique*, XXVII (1926), 140–54. Madeleine Pardo, "Remarques sur l'*Atalaya* de l'Archiprêtre de Talavera," *Romania*, LXXXVIII (1967), 350–98.

21. See Ramón Menéndez Pidal, ed., *Primera Crónica General de España* (Madrid: Gredos, 1955), I, 312–14.

22. In del Piero, *Dos escritores*, p. 99.

23. See Menéndez Pidal, II, 413–14.

Selected Bibliography

PRIMARY SOURCES

Editions of Works by Alfonso Martínez de Toledo

Arcipreste de Talavera. Edited by Mario Penna. Torino: Rosenberg & Sellier, 1955. Excellent introduction. Good text. Appendix contains Book III of *De Amore.*

Arcipreste de Talavera. Barcelona: Zeus, 1968. Useless.

Arcipreste de Talavera. Edited by C. Pastor Sanz. Madrid: EMESA, 1971. Poor text, poor introduction.

Arcipreste de Talavera, corvacho, o reprobación del amor mundano. Edited by C. Pérez Pastor. Sociedad de Bibliófilos Españoles, 35. Madrid: M. Tello, 1901. Very good text. Important introduction.

Arcipreste de Talavera o corbacho. Edited by Joaquín González Muela. Madrid: Castalia, 1970. Good introduction and text. Readily available.

Arcipreste de Talavera, o sea el corbacho. Edited by Lesley Byrd Simpson. Berkeley: University of California Press, 1939. Transcription of Contreras manuscript.

Corbacho o reprobación del amor mundano. Edited by F. C. Sainz de Robles. Madrid: Círculo de Amigos de la Historia, 1974. Poor text, poor introduction.

Corvacho, o reprobación del amor mundano. Edited by Martín de Riquer. Barcelona: Selecciones Bibliófilas, 1949. Good text and critical observations.

De los vicios de las malas mujeres y complexiones de los hombres. Edited by E. Barriobero y Herrán. 2 vols. Madrid: Mundo Latino, 1931. The very worst edition.

Libro del Arcipreste de Talavera. Edited by José Rogerio Sánchez. Madrid: Hernando, n.d. [1929?]. Introduction is a critical gem.

Little Sermons on Sin (Arcipreste de Talavera). Translated by Lesley Byrd Simpson. Berkeley: University of California Press, 1959. Excellent English translation: Parts I, II, and III.

San Ildefonso de Toledo a través de la pluma del Arcipreste de Talavera. Edited by José Madoz. Biblioteca de Antiguos Escritores Cristianos Españoles, 2. Madrid: CSIC, 1943. Good text and introduction. Contains Martínez's translation of *De Virginitate Sanctae Mariae Contra Tres Infideles.*

Vidas de San Ildefonso y San Isidoro. Edited by J. Madoz y Moleres. Clásicos Castellanos, 134. Madrid: Espasa-Calpe, 1962. Readily available. Does not, however, contain Martínez's *De la virginidat de Nuestra Señora.*

SECONDARY SOURCES

Books and Articles dealing with Alfonso Martínez de Toledo

ALONSO, DÁMASO. *De los siglos oscuros al de oro.* 2nd ed. Madrid: Gredos, 1964, pp. 125–36. Concentrates on style of *Arcipreste de Talavera.*

AMADOR DE LOS RÍOS, JOSÉ. *Historia crítica de la literatura española.* 7 vols. Madrid: Fernández Cancela, 1861–65, VI, 277–85. First study to discuss sources. Out of date.

BARADAT, A. "Qui a inspiré son livre à l'Archiprêtre de Talavera?" In *Mélanges offerts à M. le Professeur Henri Gavel.* Toulouse: Privat, 1948, pp. 3–12. Argues that Juan de Ausim is Aeneas Silvius Piccolomini.

BELL, AUBREY F. G. "The Archpriest of Talavera." *Bulletin of Spanish Studies,* V (1928), 60–67. Descriptive, but does provide some literary insights.

BOUDET, THÉODORE JOSEPH, COMTE DE PUYMAIGRE. *La Cour littéraire de don Juan II.* 2 vols. Paris: Franck, 1873, I, 156–66. First to recognize the relationship of *Corbacho* to *Celestina.* Still contains interesting observations.

CICERI, MARCELLA. "Rilettura del manoscritto escurialense dell' *Arcipreste de Talavera.*" *Cultura Neolatina,* XXXI (1971), 225–35. A list of corrections for Simpson's transcription of the Contreras manuscript.

CIROT, GEORGES. "Note sur l'*Atalaya* de l'Archiprêtre de Talavera." In *Homenaje a Menéndez Pidal.* 6 vols. Madrid: Hernando, 1925, I, 355–69. Describes ms. Egerton 287 and points out parallels of last chapters and *Generaciones y semblanzas.*

FARINELLI, ARTURO. "Note sul Boccaccio in Ispagna nell' Età Media." *Archiv für das Studium der neuren Sprachen und Literaturen,* CXIV (1905), 397–429; CXV (1905), 368–88; CXVI (1906), 67–96; CXVII (1906), 114–41. Discusses Boccaccio's influence on Martínez de Toledo.

———. "Note sulla fortuna del *Corbaccio* nella Spagna medievale." In *Bausteine zur romanischen Philologies Festgabe für Adolfo*

Mussafia. Halle: Niemeyer, 1905, pp. 440–60. Believes *Corbaccio* might have influenced the *Archpriest.* Textual comparisons are not convincing.

García Rey, Verardo. "El Arcipreste de Talavera, Alonso Martínez de Toledo." *Revista de la Biblioteca, Archivo y Museo del Ayuntamiento de Madrid,* V (1928), 298–306. Very important biographical findings.

Gerli, E. Michael. "*Ars Praedicandi* and the Structure of *Arcipreste de Talavera,* Part I." *Hispania,* LVIII (1975), 430–41. See Chapter 4, section I, of this study.

———. "Monólogo y diálogo en el *Arcipreste de Talavera.*" *Revista de Literatura,* XXXV (1969), 107–11. See Chapter 3 of this study.

González Muela, Joaquín. *El infinitivo en el "Corbacho" del Arcipreste de Talavera.* Colección Filológica, 8. Granada: Universidad de Granada, 1954. Studies Latinate use of infinitives.

Martínez López, Enrique. *Alfonso Martínez de Toledo, insuficiente arcipreste.* Paraiba, Brazil: João Pessoa, 1955. Survey of life, text, and themes. Very rare.

Menéndez y Pelayo, Marcelino. *Orígenes de la novela.* 4 vols. Madrid: CSIC, 1943, I, 176–91. Critical milestone.

Ornstein, Jacob. "La misoginia y el profeminismo en la literatura castellana." *Revista de Filología Hispánica,* III (1941), 219–32. Surveys literary antifeminism in Castile up to 1500.

Pardo, Madeleine. "Remarques sur l'*Atalaya* de l'Archiprêtre de Talavera." *Romania,* LXXXVIII (1967), 350–98. Discusses influence of Pérez de Guzmán, the *Abreviación del halconero,* and *Anales* of Garci Sánchez on last chapters of *Atalaya.*

Piero, Raúl del. *Dos escritores de la baja Edad Media castellana (Pedro de Veragüe y el Arcipreste de Talavera, Cronista Real).* Supplement of the *Boletín de la Real Academia Española,* XXIII (Madrid, 1970). First ten chapters of *Atalaya* are edited here.

———. "El Arcipreste de Talavera y Juan de Ausim." *Bulletin Hispanique,* LXII (1960), 125–35. Believes Juan de Ausim is Nicolaus Auximanus Picenus. Not convincing.

———. "Sobre el autor y la fecha del *Invencionario.*" *Hispanic Review,* XXX (1962), 12–20. Denies Martínez is author of *Invencionario.*

———. "La *Corónica de Mahomad* del Arcipreste de Talavera." *Nueva Revista de Filología Hispánica,* XIV (1960), 21–50. Edits chapter 16 of *Atalaya.*

———. "La tradición textual de la *Atalaya de las corónicas* del

Arcipreste de Talavera." *Publications of the Modern Language Association*, LXXXI (1966), 12–22. Establishes manuscript tradition of *Atalaya*. Very important study.

———. "El *Vencimiento del mundo*: autor, fecha, estructura." *Nueva Revista de Filología Hispánica*, XV (1961), 377–92. Skeptically discusses possibility Martínez wrote *Vencimiento*.

RICHTHOFEN, ERICH F. VON. "Alfonso Martínez de Toledo und sein *Arcipreste de Talauera*, ein kastilisches Prosawerk des 15. Jahrhunderts." *Zeitschrift für romanische Philologie*, LXI (1941), 417–537. The most comprehensive and important study on Martínez de Toledo.

———. "El *Corbacho*: las interpolaciones y la deuda de la *Celestina*." In *Homenaje a Rodríguez-Moñino*. 2 vols. Madrid: Castalia, 1966, II, 115–20. Discusses influence of *Corbacho* on the *Celestina*. Important for what it suggests.

———. "Neue Veröffentlichungen zum Werk des Erzpriesters von Talavera." *Zeitschrift für romanische Philologie*, LXVI (1950), 383–84. Describes studies on Martínez published between 1941 and 1950.

———. "Zum Wortgebrauch des Erzpriesters von Talavera." *Zeitschrift für romanische Philologie*, LXXII (1956), 108–14. Linguistic study; analyzes dialectalisms and vocabulary.

ROIG, JAUME. *El espejo*. Edited and translated by R. Miquel y Planas. Barcelona: Orbis, 1936–42. Editor relates *Corbacho* to Roig's work in introduction. Discusses antifeminism of both.

ROTUNDA, D. P. "The *Corvacho* version of the Husband Locked Out Story." *Romanic Review*, XXVI (1935), 121–27. Attempts to determine origin of version in one of *Corbacho's* interpolations.

STEIGER, ARNALD. "Contribución al estudio del vocabulario del *Corbacho*." *Boletín de la Real Academia Española*, IX (1922), 503–25; X (1923), 26–54, 158–88, 275–93. The most important vocabulary study.

WHITBOURN, CHRISTINE J. *The "Arcipreste de Talavera" and the Literature of Love*. Occasional Papers in Modern Languages, 7. Hull: University of Hull, 1970. Important study.

Index